BEN H████'S
SECRET
FUNDAMENTAL

BEN HOGAN'S SECRET FUNDAMENTAL

What He Never Told the World

Larry Miller

TRIUMPH
BOOKS

Library of Congress Cataloging-in-Publication Data available upon request

This book is available in quantity at special discounts for your group or organization. For further information, contact:

Triumph Books LLC
814 North Franklin Street
Chicago, Illinois 60610
(312) 337-0747
www.triumphbooks.com

Printed in U.S.A.
ISBN: 978-1-62937-282-2
Design by Amy Carter
Photography by Kelly Redfield Whitworth

CONTENTS

PREFACE

THE GOLF SWING is a beautiful but baffling blend of art and science.

The art of it is in the creative ways that we use the science.

Modern technology has provided us with the tools to pin down the science, and then it is up to us to work with that knowledge in our own individual, creative ways.

Most people think that Ben Hogan was the ultimate technician, a human machine, when it came to swinging a golf club and striking a golf ball. And while he did achieve great ability to repeat an incredibly effective swing time after time, he was at the same time a creative genius in that he *used* the science of the swing that he'd discovered to craft an array of golf shots that bordered on poetry in motion.

In this book you will learn the hard science of what Hogan found—his true secret—and then it will be up to you to decide how you want to use it for your own game.

In doing so, reinforced with drills to help you along, you will gain the ability to *control* the golf ball.

You will also learn Hogan's secrets of course management, and his secrets of concentration, all of which will result in greater enjoyment and lower scores.

Ben Hogan is legendary, intriguing, and mysterious. It's a combination that has contributed to Hogan being the most interesting golfer in the long history of the game.

Aside from his amazing competitive record, Hogan's secretive and solitary personality provokes wonder and devotion among thousands, perhaps millions, of golfers worldwide who attempt to unlock Hogan's secret code of how to swing a golf club and strike a golf ball.

Hogan himself fueled this intrigue, mainly because he openly declared that he had a "secret," one that he never publicly revealed.

Many top professionals have speculated on what they thought Hogan's secret might be, but those speculations were not supported by any revelations from Hogan himself.

Until now.

I've always been hesitant to write this book, mainly because Hogan demanded that what he shared with a select few not be shared with the general golfing population. This was not because he wanted to be secretive, but because he was afraid that what he said would probably be distorted and therefore misunderstood. He was afraid that if that happened, it would cause much more harm than good.

Hogan, while he was still competitive, only seriously mentored two top professionals, Ken Venturi and Tommy Bolt. And, according to Tommy, only he and Venturi were entrusted with the whole of what Hogan had discovered about the golf swing. Not coincidentally, those two, largely due to Hogan's influence and tutelage, combined for 33 professional victories, including two major championships and eight top-five finishes in majors.

Both Venturi and Bolt are World Golf Hall of Fame members.

Tommy Bolt was my teacher during my very early twenties, before I became a PGA Tour player. Bolt learned from Hogan, and I learned from Bolt. Tommy shared with me many things that he learned from Ben Hogan, many things that have never before appeared in any of the numerous writings on or by Hogan.

Staying loyal to his teachers' wishes, Tommy included me in the "code" of privacy, asking that I not share what I learned as long as the principals were alive, and, unless, as Hogan said to Bolt, "You find a worthy and trusted protégé."

But, since Ben Hogan's passing, and the passing of his wife, Valerie, several people have come forward to write about their firsthand relationships with Hogan, feeling that the veil of secrecy could be lifted without violating the privacy of the man.

Bolt always said that he'd like to see the whole of Hogan's discoveries put forth in such a way as to help all golfers improve their swings, but that it had to be done "sometime in the future," after Hogan and Valerie were gone. He also stressed Hogan's concerns about what he'd found being "distorted" or misrepresented.

Since the passing of Hogan and his wife, and the passing of Tommy Bolt, books began to appear by people who had close relationships with Ben Hogan through golf, social interaction, or business interests. And for decades now, every Tom, Dick, and Harry has speculated on what his true secret was. I have long felt that if Hogan's secret were presented properly it could help thousands of golfers improve their performance and increase their enjoyment of the game.

After reading a bunch of these books, and reading all of the speculations about what various people thought his "secret" was, I became more and more convinced that the time was right to once and for all put an end to the guessing.

This is why I have decided to write this book. Tommy Bolt told me exactly what Hogan's "secret" was, and I intend to present it in such a way as to hopefully eliminate any chance of misrepresentation. I will also offer advice on how average golfers can implement Hogan's teachings in order to benefit their own performance. No one can swing the club like Ben Hogan. He was somewhat of a freak of nature in the way that he could produce and retain "lag" in the swing (due mainly to his unique physical characteristics). However, his swing principles will be of great benefit to anyone who will put forth the effort to diligently and properly work with them.

Tommy Bolt was old-school. He was straightforward, he was serious-minded, and when he spoke, it had substance.

Everything he taught me and told me came straight from his teacher, Ben Hogan. And with Tommy there were no embellishments, no distortions.

Tommy said that without Hogan's help he would have been relegated to a career as a carpenter, and not the world-class U.S. Open Champion and Hall of Fame member that he became.

Both Bolt and Venturi paid homage to Hogan for his mentorship in print, publicly. Both were asked by Valerie to be honorary pallbearers at Ben's funeral.

Both men took the baton from Hogan and ran with it magnificently. Anyone who was privileged to experience Ben Hogan up close and personal was better for it in so many ways, and likewise, if you study the golfer and the man, you too will benefit on and off the course.

—Larry Miller, PGA Professional

ACKNOWLEDGMENTS

HAVING BEEN IMMERSED in the art and science of golf for 60 years, it's difficult, if not impossible, to recall every positive influence that's come my way during this journey.

I call this journey "the endless pursuit of perfection that can never be attained."

Of course, there were early influences. My late dad introduced me to the game, and along with my late mom went the extra mile to encourage and support my growing interest.

Then there were the early teachers, long gone from this world, whose emphasis was on the basic fundamentals of grip, stance, posture, etc.

As I developed as a player, the lessons broadened into the intricacies and complexities of performing an efficient golf swing, a never-ending quest that continues to this day.

My career branched into two, for me, interconnected directions, first as a player and then as a teacher.

I've always been a keen student of the game and of the golf swing.

I've learned from other players, from other teachers, and most of all from the multitudes of students that I've helped through the years.

Just like Harvey Penick, I've learned something from every student I've taught.

A great teacher must possess three qualities: diagnostic abilities, communication skills (which includes "people reading"), and healing knowledge. Only the very best possess all three.

The first teacher who introduced me to the intricacies was Jim Hart, a former PGA Tour player and my first boss in the golf business at Lakewood Country Club in New Orleans.

Jim not only was generous with his time and knowledge in educating me in the ways of playing and teaching, but made sure that I had lots of time to practice and play. Very unselfish and rare for a boss.

Then there was Freddie Haas, a former Ryder Cup player who played in the Hogan era. Freddie was the one who, by winning the Memphis Open, snapped Byron Nelson's incredible streak of 11 consecutive tournament wins.

Freddie, a fellow New Orleanian, was always willing to share his wealth of knowledge, especially concerning putting, a vital aspect of the game that he excelled at. Arnold Palmer once said that Freddie was the best putter in the game.

Then of course there was Tommy Bolt, whose mentorship really pushed me to the level of a PGA Tour player and without whom this book would not exist.

I owe all of those teachers, and others from my distant past, unpayable amounts of gratitude.

Moving to the personal side, it's equally hard to single out friends and family whose influences have been instrumental to my continuing education.

To my close circle of friends—you know who you are—thanks for your loyal friendship and guidance.

The folks at Triumph Books were astute enough to see the importance of this book, no doubt fueled by the fact that they had recently published a wonderful, comprehensive book about Ben Hogan.

I was highly impressed with the staff at Triumph, and with the professionalism and enthusiasm they display consistently through the process of creating a book.

Michelle Bruton, my editor, has been a pleasure to work with, and I'm sure that her golfer husband will experience lower scores after implementing the techniques within!

I've been excited about this book ever since my initial conversation with Mitch Rogatz, publisher and president of Triumph Books, who had an immediate vision of how this project might progress, and has guided it in the right direction.

To Ben Hogan, for his mastery and discoveries, and to Bolt, Hogan's protégé, who took me into his confidence and shared all he'd learned, I owe this book's existence.

I have three sons, Ryan, Jeffrey, and Jonathan, and one grandson, Cameron, and they all, in their own ways, give me energy just because I know they're there.

Last but most important, I owe everything that I've learned about honor, integrity, and grace to Connie, my guiding star.

Over the past 28 years I've witnessed her incredible heart at work as she unselfishly makes every life she touches better and brighter.

And, I might proudly add, she is one hell of a golfer, with 10 club championships and nearly 20 USGA tournament appearances to her credit—a very talented lady in many, many ways.

INTRODUCTION

WHY IS GOLF such a difficult game? Millions of beginners—and many more millions of longtime players—have probably asked themselves this question. It's especially mystifying when they watch a world-class player swing the club and strike the ball with what appears to be effortless ease.

First of all, many people take up the game without quality instruction. They either copy a friend or just start hitting balls based on what they may have seen, read, or watched. They develop bad swing habits right from the start, and the longer they play with these bad habits, the more ingrained they become.

World-class players start with quality instruction and typically start very young. Then they spend countless hours, day after day, practicing *good* swing habits. Especially today, with the technology involved, young players never have had a bad swing. They've never had to "undo" swing flaws.

So when a golfer has gone months, or even years with bad swing habits, he or she develops compensations and adjustments to make up for these flaws. These compensations require perfect timing, and some days they work fairly well, and some days not at all. It's hit or miss.

Then there are some world-class players who have swing flaws of their own, so how are they able to still perform on such a level?

The answer to that question lies in the fact that these players have practiced compensating for their flaws for many years, hitting literally millions of balls to perfect their adjustments. But because they rely on timing and hand-eye coordination, even *they* have bad days when their compensations are a bit off.

What Ben Hogan discovered, his "secret," enabled him to create a golf swing free from compensations or adjustments. Hogan, unlike any other player in the history of the game, never had bad days when it came to striking and controlling the golf ball. Hitting 15 to 18 greens a round in regulation became a constant for him.

Sure, Hogan hit a bad shot or two in most rounds. But they were few and far between. After all, he was human. But most of his shots were very, very good, featured by pinpoint accuracy.

The beauty of what Hogan discovered is that the secret to the most efficient way to swing a golf club is rooted in simple geometry.

And the beauty of this book is that by practicing the drills presented here, you, the average golfer, can break those bad habits and replace them with Ben Hogan's secret fundamental.

These drills will bring you closer and closer to the true geometry of a perfect swing. Your golf swing and your ball striking will get better and better as you perform repetitions using the drills.

It doesn't matter if you are a beginner, weekend golfer, top amateur, or touring pro: you can improve your technique and become more consistent as you free yourself from compensations and in-swing adjustments that ensure inconsistency and rob the swing of power.

Good luck—on and off the course!

Note: All references to the golf swing or grip assume right-handedness. For lefties, simply reverse the reference.

MY HISTORY

I STARTED PLAYING golf when I was eight years old. Like many others, my dad got me interested by bringing me along when he played with his friends at the old No. 2 course at City Park in New Orleans. It was known as "the little course."

At the time (the mid-to-late 1950s), the New Orleans Open was played on the No. 1 course at City Park. In those days, the No. 1 course was top-notch, and Ben Hogan, Byron Nelson, Sam Snead, Arnold Palmer, and all of the golfing elite of that era walked those fairways.

At first, my golf game was limited to chipping balls around the tee boxes when my dad's group had to wait on the group ahead. I quickly became hooked when I realized that if I did things properly, I could *control* the ball's direction as well as its distance.

As I began playing and developing, I gradually started playing on the big No. 1 course, and by the time I was 15 I was shooting par most of the time.

When I was 17, I won the City Junior Championship at Timberlane Country Club in New Orleans by 15 strokes.

When I graduated from Holy Cross High School in New Orleans, I was offered a full golf scholarship to Loyola University. That next spring, I was the low amateur in the New Orleans Open, which had moved to Lakewood Country Club. I turned pro in 1967 and became the assistant pro under Jim Hart at Lakewood Country Club in New Orleans, and set my sights on eventually playing on the PGA Tour. Jim Hart helped accelerate my development by sharing his knowledge of the golf swing, teaching me *how* to teach, and encouraging me to develop good practice habits. He was always supportive of my playing and never just stuck me in the golf shop like so many bosses do. I owe him a huge debt of gratitude.

So at Lakewood I learned how to teach the game, and teaching has been a huge part of my golfing life ever since.

The next year I left Lakewood for a teaching job at Racine Country Club in Racine, Wisconsin, and that is where this story begins.

MEETING TOMMY BOLT

THE HEAD PROFESSIONAL at Racine Country Club who hired me was Bob Ford from Georgetown, South Carolina. Bob had a close friend who happened to be a close friend of none other than Tommy Bolt, the 1958 U.S. Open champion. Tommy had retired from the Tour and lived in Sarasota, Florida, where he owned a par-3 course called the Golden Tee.

Bolt still played almost every day with his buddies at Longboat Key, a great, tough course in Sarasota. Tommy and his buddies would meet for lunch, have a couple of pops, and then play nine holes on good weather days.

My boss, Bob Ford, was a really good player himself, and he knew my aspirations. He and I played a lot of golf together, and we were pretty evenly matched most of the time.

One day, after I had shot 28–35, 63, which was nine under par and a course record, Bob asked me if I would like to go down to Sarasota and have Tommy Bolt have a look at my game.

I was planning to begin my professional playing career that winter down in Florida anyway, and naturally I jumped at the chance to have one of the best players in the history of the game help me.

So Bob set it up for me to go down and meet Bolt as soon as our season in Wisconsin ended.

For the initial meeting, my dad and I drove down to Sarasota, and as instructed I checked in at the golf shop at Longboat Key at the appointed time.

The assistant behind the counter told me to go on down to the practice tee and warm up. "Mr. Bolt will be down shortly to meet you."

"Shortly" became about 45 minutes and I just kept hitting shots, glancing back toward the clubhouse after every shot or two.

Suddenly, a golf cart pulled up and Bolt was sitting there. He said, "Are you Larry?" I said, "Yes, sir," and started to walk over to shake hands. I got about halfway before he said, "Just go ahead and hit a few shots." So I hit a few drivers and he said, "Good balance, really good tempo." And he left. I turned and looked at my dad, and he just shrugged his shoulders. So I started hitting shots again, thinking he was coming right back, but he never did.

Eventually I went back to the pro shop. The head pro was there, and I told him what happened. He laughed and said that Bolt meant that he really liked my tempo and balance, and that I should continue practicing with those two things in mind. Then he said that I should show up the next day, same time, and that Bolt would come back out to see me.

In the days to come I learned that Bolt's reputation for being cantankerous and short-tempered was well-deserved, but for the record, there was a warm and caring man buried deep inside. As I got to know him and as he got to know me, he shared more and more of his knowledge, although I mostly had to glean it from watching, listening, and reading between the lines.

Bolt was not particularly articulate, and he had little patience for actually teaching in the traditional sense.

What he did do, however, which was worth its weight in gold, was let me play nine holes every day with him and his cronies. He must have seen some potential in me, but true to his personality he never said so.

Every now and then, after our nine-hole, late-afternoon outings, he would invite me into the grill room for a drink or two.

Eventually his buddies would head home and then he'd talk. And that was where the *real* learning took place.

Whenever he would talk about the golf swing, he would almost always start by saying, "Hogan said..." and it was obvious that to him Hogan's word was the golfing Bible. And why not? Ben Hogan was the greatest striker of the golf ball who ever played the game, and that opinion is shared by every great player who ever witnessed his mastery firsthand.

Those rounds that I played with Tommy back then really opened my eyes as to just how good world-class players are. He was way past his prime, but you'd never know it watching him hit golf shots.

One day in the early evening, I was on the practice tee hitting drivers when he drove up in his golf cart. He was dressed for dinner, wearing a sport coat, dress slacks, and leather loafers.

He walked up and took my driver and looked at it, and then waggled it a few times to get the feel. He told me that it felt pretty good, and then teed up a ball. Without even a practice swing, he drilled one dead straight about 260 yards. With a sport coat on and street shoes. I couldn't believe it. He got back in the cart without saying anything and drove off, as if what he just did was nothing special. Have you ever tried to swing with a sport coat on? It's like wearing a straitjacket! The guy was immensely talented.

The other notable thing about playing with Bolt was witnessing the grace with which he swung. Explosive, powerful, efficient, and yet very graceful. If you watch videos of Hogan, Nelson, Snead, and others of that era, you'll see the same element of grace in their swings.

That's missing in the modern stars. The modern pros are efficient, explosive, and very powerful, but for a few exceptions you don't see the fluid, graceful rhythm that those guys had.

I believe that there are two reasons for that.

First, weight training. Those guys like Hogan, Bolt, Nelson, and Snead, and even a little later when Ken Venturi played, never touched a dumbbell. They weren't as strong as the modern players, but they were more flexible.

Plus, the game has changed. The courses have become much longer because the equipment has required it. The ball goes farther and the clubs hit them farther. And it's a vicious cycle. Every time technology produces a club and ball that travels farther, the golf holes must get longer to offer a challenge to the player.

But the geometry of an efficient, repeatable, powerful golf swing has not changed!

That brings me back to Hogan and his secret.

Some have said that Hogan himself was the secret. Others said that "he dug it out of the dirt," as Ben himself was known to say. But while true that he was unique physically and also true that he practiced more than anyone in the history of the game, his secret to ball striking goes a lot deeper than that.

Hogan had a very analytical mind, and he carefully calculated his every action and every word. So it's no surprise that he came up with profound ideas regarding the golf swing—ideas that he proved valid by his performance.

The late Freddie Haas, from New Orleans, was a PGA Tour player during Hogan's time. Freddie was best known for winning the Memphis Open and snapping Byron Nelson's amazing streak of 11 consecutive PGA Tour wins in 1945.

Freddie wound up winning five times on the PGA Tour, and notched three top 10s in majors. He represented the United States on the 1953 Ryder Cup team.

Connie and I were close to Freddie, and I consider him one of my important early mentors. We competed against each other in lots of tournaments in the PGA Gulf States Section and played lots of practice rounds and social rounds together. In his later years Connie and I would sometimes play with him at New Orleans Country Club. We would play nine holes in the afternoon, and he insisted we play a scramble. I think he liked playing from Connie's great tee shots, which had a head start from the ladies' tee!

One day during one of those outings I said to him, "Freddie, I've never asked you this, but I'm curious. All the stories about Hogan's ball striking—have they been embellished and exaggerated through the years?"

Well, first of all, let me tell you what kind of guy Freddie was. There was no gray area. Just black or white. No theatrics or histrionics. No embellishments. If he told you something, you could take it to the bank. So I knew he'd give me a straight and true answer.

He said, "No, no exaggeration whatsoever. Sure, he would hit the occasional bad shot, but nine out of 10 times he would play exceptional shots. He could place the ball within 5 yards or less of where he wanted it much of the time. He had much more control of his shots than any of us ever dreamed of. He reminded me of a master billiard player, the way that he would set himself up for the next shot."

Hearing that made me think back to what I learned from Tommy Bolt, and I knew then that Hogan really had found important keys to swinging a golf club and controlling a golf ball.

HOGAN'S CODE OF SECRECY

REGARDING HOGAN'S "CODE of secrecy," he was very, very serious about it. Bolt said, as have several others, that to ever hope to be a trusted friend of Hogan's, you better make sure that your word or your handshake was your bond. An unbreakable bond.

This is why, after their passing, all of these books have come out by people who knew Ben and Valerie, giving various accounts of their relationships. All of these books, the one you're holding included, would never have been published while Ben and Valerie Hogan were alive.

Likewise, with Tommy's passing, I now feel free to recall and share what I learned during my time with him all those years ago.

The Hogan-Bolt-Venturi Connection

It's been said that the best relationships are formed when the persons involved are either very much alike or completely different. With Ben Hogan, Ken Venturi, and Tommy Bolt, this theory is certainly true.

Venturi was very much like Hogan. He was an insatiable practicer, a super hard worker. He was serious and quiet. He overcame an extreme stuttering problem to become a renowned television commentator. His shyness, especially early in his life, probably stemmed from the self-consciousness caused by his speech impediment. Hogan also overcame early adversity of great magnitude, witnessing as a young boy his father's suicide.

Hogan surely connected with Venturi on a personal level given their similar personalities, and then when he saw the raw talent and work ethic that Venturi displayed, decided to take him under his wing.

Venturi gave Hogan, along with Byron Nelson, all the credit for helping him develop into a top world-class player.

When Venturi won the U.S. Open at Congressional, he staggered through the final eighteen holes, battling severe heat exhaustion to the extent that he nearly collapsed before finishing.

That courageous effort mirrored the same level of will and determination displayed by Hogan during his comeback from the horrific car wreck that nearly killed him in 1949. He was told that he would probably never play golf again, and yet in 1950 he came back to win the Los Angeles Open and then the U.S. Open on legs that constantly hurt.

Tommy Bolt was the antithesis of Hogan. He'd rather have a cocktail than spend more than an hour on the practice tee. He was loud, boisterous, gruff, and grumpy, and sometimes vulgar. He had little patience for anything that perturbed him. But he had incredible natural talent. He had power and he had grace. He was not at all a mechanic. He was an artist.

Once Hogan took Tommy under his wing, he blossomed into a more finished talent, and went on to become one of the best players in the world, and himself a U.S. Open Champion.

In Tommy's first book, published in 1969, the dedication is to "Ben Hogan, the only teacher I've ever had." And in his second book, published in 1999, the book begins with a two-page statement about Hogan, and how he, Bolt, would never have even made it to the PGA Tour without Hogan's teachings and guidance.

I believe that Hogan took a liking to Tommy for two reasons. First, he recognized and appreciated the raw talent and potential. Second, Hogan, unbeknownst to many, had a great sense of humor and probably got a real kick out of Tommy's "character" personality. Hogan liked characters, as long as they were sincere and not trying to con him.

And I'd like to add something about Tommy Bolt that I learned in the years I knew him—that there was one thing, after all, that he had in common with Ben Hogan: a huge heart. That fact was mostly unknown to those who were outside of the two men's inner circles.

Hogan and Bolt, the Men

When Tommy Bolt came out of the Army he was already a very good player, but not yet a world-class player. Ben Hogan took a liking to Bolt, perhaps because they were so completely different. Again, the old adage that very often opposites attract proves true. Hogan was reserved, serious, very proper, composed, and focused. Bolt was brash, never composed, rarely serious, and certainly not inclined to social grace. But his golf swing was the picture of it.

Perhaps Hogan, seeing the raw talent and intrigued by the blatant differences between them, decided to take Tommy under his wing.

I never did ask Tommy much about how the mentorship began, but he did talk about how Hogan put him on the right track by radically changing his grip right from the start of their teacher-student relationship.

There was no telling who Hogan decided to help or when. I believe that it had a lot to do with the potential student's work ethic, desire, and character. He seemed drawn to some who were very serious and reserved like himself, and yet he also seemed enamored with some of life's real characters.

When he decided to help LPGA Tour player Kris Tschetter, it was because he noticed her work ethic and dedication to getting better.

He would carefully size up a potential beneficiary of his knowledge to make sure that first, the student was worthy in terms of his or her potential and willingness to work, and second that he or she was the type of person who possessed integrity and could be trusted not to carelessly spread around what they'd learned from him. Hogan was extremely protective of his knowledge, because he was fearful that it would be misrepresented and consequently distorted over time. The result would be harmful instead of helpful, so he was very careful when it came to trusting anyone with whom he shared his knowledge.

If he felt that you'd violated his confidence, he'd have nothing to do with you.

Hogan's code of decency, respect, and etiquette was one that he steadfastly adhered to, without exception. He did not tolerate "off-color" language in front of women, and he did not suffer fools, not even for a second. Here's an example of the seriousness with which he stuck to his guns: I recently was playing in a little event at the Ocean Reef Club in Key Largo, Florida. Waiting to tee off, an older gentleman who was in the threesome behind my group saw my Hogan golf bag, monogrammed The Secret, Spring 2017, and approached me.

He asked me about this book, which I was in the process of writing. Then he told me he had a Hogan story. He said that he'd had some oil dealings down in Texas years earlier.

It seems that he'd had a close friend in Fort Worth who happened to be an oilman and who had been among Hogan's "inner circle" at Shady Oaks. This guy apparently had been in some oil deals with Hogan, and must have been pretty close to Hogan because he was one of the few who'd had a permanent seat at Hogan's table in the grill at Shady Oaks.

It seems that this oilman had a grandson who was attending college in New Jersey and who apparently was a really good college player with aspirations to play professionally. This gentleman described the grandson, whom he knew because the team played and practiced at his club, as "cocky and gregarious."

The kid knew that his grandfather was a friend of Hogan's and thought that this gave him entrée into being able to contact Hogan. So the kid called the Ben Hogan Golf Company in Fort Worth and gave his name, and mentioned that he's so-and-so's grandson.

Naturally, seeing this message, Hogan accepted the call. The kid then proceeded to tell Hogan that he intended to turn pro after college and join the Tour, and that he understood that Hogan had a "secret" and would he mind telling him what the secret was.

The way this gentleman described Hogan's response to me was that the only thing the kid heard was the sound of a click as the phone was hung up.

I can only imagine the reprimand that that kid received from his grandfather, but at the same time I can just see Hogan and the grandfather having a good laugh at that table at Shady Oaks.

There's no way to know for sure, but I'd bet that eventually, quietly, Hogan did something for his friend's grandson.

His personal stamp on anything, from the golf clubs he produced at the Ben Hogan Golf Company to the lessons he gave to selected individuals, was golden to Hogan. He went to great lengths to protect the integrity of that personal stamp.

Ken Venturi and Tommy Bolt were very different personalities, and yet they both met Hogan's criteria for qualifying as a protégé—Venturi with his work ethic, desire, and dedication to his teacher, and Bolt with his incredible natural gifts and his willingness to do what his teacher demanded, even in the face of frustration and the absence of instant gratification. He knew that what Hogan was teaching him was absolutely correct and would ultimately result in great improvement. Such was his respect for Hogan the man and Hogan the golfer.

Ben Hogan was not just private with his golf. He kept private many of the charitable things that he did for those people whom he deemed deserving of his charitable acts. The stories have become legends of the times that he heard of someone's misfortune and quietly lent a hand. Those close to him, of course, knew about these things, but respectful of his wishes, they kept them private. Only after his death did these stories come out.

So you might say that Hogan's greatest secret was the way that he hid his warm, sensitive, caring side from the public eye. Most likely he did this so as not to erode the focused, single-minded tactician that he had to be on the golf course and on the practice tee. The two Hogans had to be separated by this wall in order for both to be free to operate efficiently and with undisturbed attention. If the perception was that he was a softie, what would that do to his steely-eyed golfing persona?

About Swing Changes

Too many aspiring golfers give up too soon on swing changes when those changes don't return fast positive results. They revert to their comfort zones and get caught in an endless loop of quick fixes that never last. When you make a change in technique, you must be willing to endure enough repetitions in order for the change to become ingrained. The only way to form a new habit is for the new habit to be repeated enough times for it to supplant the old one as the automatic action.

The hardest thing when getting instruction is to trust the teaching. An important consideration when seeking instruction is to research the lineage. When considering a teacher, you must find out who that teacher's teacher was. It's sort of like with football coaches. When the lineage reveals a quality "bloodline," the trust factor grows. Then, when instant gratification doesn't occur, you're much more likely to trust the teaching and stick with the program.

Despite already being a very good player, Bolt had an extremely strong grip—strong meaning that his hands were turned to the right, with three to four knuckles showing on his left hand. Because of this, whenever he tried to really release his hands hard at impact, he was prone to hitting the occasional "duck hook," a shot that often results in disaster as it ducks abruptly to the left. Even if the shot stays in bounds it usually ends up in trouble, behind a tree or in a lake or pond or some other type of hazard.

Bolt said that Hogan changed his grip to a neutral one, where the palms of both hands were perpendicular to the target line, and with only two knuckles visible on the left hand.

Hogan told him that they could progress no further until he could hit the ball straight with that grip.

Of course, if you've ever undergone a drastic grip change, you know how traumatic it is at first. Tommy said that it took him weeks before he could hit a shot that didn't fly way to the right of his target. He said that he almost gave up and reverted to his comfort zone—the strong grip.

But he persevered, knowing that Hogan was right. And then, suddenly, it took. He started hitting solid, straight shots. And the harder he swung, the farther and straighter the shots flew.

And after that grip change, the first of Hogan's lessons, Tommy's career took off.

If you revisit Hogan's *Five Lessons*, you'll see that the book begins: "Good golf begins with a good grip."

Tommy Bolt was a raw talent. He was short-tempered and impatient. He played the game by feel. Hogan, the opposite, had to create his swing piece by piece through endless practice. He was the consummate mechanic, the ultimate tactician.

Hogan once said that if he could put another head onto Bolt's shoulders everyone would be playing for second place. That's how talented Tommy was. I witnessed it firsthand those times that I played with him in Sarasota, Florida. He was retired and past his prime, but he could hit shots with power and grace that were amazing. Seeing how good he was made me work harder at my game, because like Hogan, I had to create my swing. Tommy was more like Sam Snead, born with a natural gift.

HOGAN'S SECRET

IN THE AUGUST 8, 1955, issue of *Life* magazine, Ben Hogan was featured in the cover story declaring that he was revealing his "secret." Many people have questioned whether or not what was revealed in that article was indeed the whole of what Hogan had found.

Mike Wright, the longtime director of golf at Shady Oaks, had many years of close contact with Hogan, and was a firsthand witness to his golfing mastery and his personality.

Wright doubted that Hogan would give away any profound secret that he had discovered, and many others agree.

Even the article in that *Life* magazine "revelation" pointed out features (such as the supposedly secret "cupped left hand") of Hogan's technique that could be found in scores of other top players, not only of that era but in modern-era players as well.

That "revelation" in *Life* magazine was one of Hogan's *own* swing secrets, but hardly an all-encompassing secret of the golf swing.

The bottom line is that Hogan, through the years, shared snippets of moves and positions that he considered to be principles of the golf swing. He did so selectively and appropriately to whom he was advising.

But according to Tommy Bolt, only he and Ken Venturi really were privy to the profound discovery that Hogan had "dug out of the dirt"—that being the basic secret, based in geometry, of how to swing a golf club most efficiently.

My belief, based on my close relationship and conversations with Bolt, is that Hogan not only realized the great potential of his two protégés, but he also came to believe that he had their trust.

Decades of Speculation

Through all these years since Ben Hogan first declared that he had a secret, hundreds of people have speculated as to what it might be. Tour players, teaching pros, and countless self-proclaimed golf swing analysts have put forth their opinions.

Numerous books have been written on the subject, and it's interesting how each analyst has a different take on what he or she perceives as the "secret."

What's also interesting is how many of the greatest players in the history of the game, and many of golf's most famous teachers, have such differing opinions on what Hogan found.

You could take any great player's golf swing and point out features of it that are integral to its effectiveness.

A particular *feature* of a golf swing—a feature that may be present in scores of other swings—can hardly be called a "secret."

A feature of a golf swing that contributes to its consistent effectiveness may be a secret to that particular swing, but that does not qualify as a profound, all-encompassing secret of the golf swing in general. And that is what Ben Hogan found.

What Hogan figured out, whether by "digging it out of the dirt" through trial and error, experimentation, or through sheer ingenuity, was much deeper and much more basic than some surface feature such as a particular position or a particular movement.

Here are just a few of the opinions of what Hogan's secret was from some famous names:

Sam Snead—"Hands never cross"

Claude Harmon—"The left hip leads"

Jimmy Demaret—"Drops his hands into 'the slot'"

Ken Venturi—"His work ethic" (that doesn't give *anything* away!)

Jody Vasquez, who shagged balls for Hogan—"The way his right leg functioned"

Dan Jenkins—"Over-clubbing"

David Leadbetter—"Cupping of the left wrist"

Walter Burkemo—"He drops his hands"

George Fazio—"Level shoulders"

Fred Gronauer—"It's his pivot"

Mike Turnesa—"Twist of the club"

Gene Sarazen—"It's pronation, a backward roll of the wrists on the backswing which opens the face of the club. Hogan does it subtly and quickly."

Harvey Penick—Harvey Penick, the legendary teacher of both average golfers and champions, wrote the top-selling sports book of all time, *Harvey Penick's Little Red Book*. It was first published in 1992 by Simon and Schuster. On page 92, in the section titled "The Mythical Perfect Swing," Harvey touches Hogan's secret geometry. In that section, he shows that he knew at least part of what Hogan had discovered. Whether or not he gained this knowledge from Hogan himself, with whom Harvey was friendly, we'll never know. But we know this much for sure: Harvey Penick came closest to figuring out Hogan's secret—the basic geometry of the perfect golf swing. Part of Penick's genius and success as a teacher of numerous champions was his ability to fit each individual into that geometry. Harvey's advice is simple, effective, and timeless.

And on and on. I could give you a hundred different observations by a hundred different players and teachers. I think you get the picture. They were, and still are, all just pointing out features of Ben Hogan's golf swing.

What's interesting is that every one of the observations are correct. Hogan did *all* of those things when he swung at a golf ball.

Whenever Hogan would pull someone aside and offer a "tip," he would tell them not to tell anyone. The reason was because it was a tip for *them*, and it might not apply to someone else who had a different type of swing or had a totally different physique.

Hogan had his own "swing keys," or "swing thoughts," which many of those people interpreted as the secret.

But deeper underneath all of his swing keys was his underlying understanding of the basic structure of the most efficient way to swing, based on geometry structured from the cornerstone of the unchanging straight line from the ball to the intended target.

Once Hogan defined and understood this geometry, he then could use it as a baseline to create any type of shot pattern that he wanted. He could play a shot dead straight or curve it left-to-right or right-to left, or any variation in fairly exact increments. He had total control over the flight of the golf ball and this was, for years, on public display.

You could say that Jack Nicklaus' secret was his flying right elbow, or that Arnie's secret was his shut clubface at the top of his backswing, or that Bobby Jones' secret was his exquisite rhythm and beautiful tempo. These were not secrets. These were *features* of their swings.

But Ben Hogan hit more good golf shots, hit more greens in regulation, and missed fewer fairways than those players ever dreamed of, great as they were. Why is that? It's not enough to say that he practiced more than anyone.

Many others since Hogan's heyday have been intense practicers, but no one, not even Tiger Woods, Phil Mickelson, Jordan Spieth, Jason Day, or Rory McIlroy has struck the golf ball so purely, so accurately, and so consistently over a long period of time like Hogan.

Plus, all of these great players have occasional, if not frequent, off days with regard to their ball striking. Many times their short games bail them out and enable them to still score well.

Hogan didn't have those off days when it came to his tee-to-green game. If anything, he was just the opposite from other top players, in that his tee-to-green game saved his scoring. His short game was not even close to being as good as any of those aforementioned players.

Lots of these modern stars hit the ball with considerably more firepower than Hogan did (though he could be very long with his driver when he wanted to), mainly because of human evolution and the tremendous advances in the technology of equipment. But no one has ever approached Hogan in the percentages of good shots hit and the numbers of greens hit in regulation.

Hogan himself, according to a number of people who knew him well, would sometimes take people aside and tell them a secret—something that would help their games. He would always say something like, "Don't tell anyone I told you this," or, "This is between you and me. I don't want to read about it in the newspaper or some magazine." He did this numerous times. Then, after his death, various people wrote about "Hogan's secret" as if they and only they had been entrusted with it.

All of these people were simply given *tips* that were appropriate for *their* golf swings. What Hogan told them had nothing to do with what took him years and thousands—no, millions—of practice balls to figure out. What he discovered through his "digging it out of the dirt" was not just a magic button tip that could instantly transform the 15 handicapper into a scratch player. What Hogan found, and the way he expressed it to Tommy Bolt, was, "the secret of the golf swing."

It consists of two vital parts. The first part is the unchanging geometry of what comprises the most efficient way to swing a golf club. The second part has to do with the human body and how its function can be optimized through the concepts of neutrality and balance.

What follows is the first part.

Ultimately, everything can be broken down and expressed in a mathematical equation. Indeed, the philosopher Gurdjieff said, "Everything in life, ultimately, is mathematics."

The universe itself is geometrical and based in mathematics. Everything is carefully balanced and constructed most likely by design. *True* astrology is most definitely all about mathematics and geometry. Flying to the moon, and Mars, is ultimately dependent on precise mathematics.

Hogan, through deep, deep practice ("digging it out of the dirt") eventually figured out that the golf swing is based mainly on *right angles and parallel lines*, with *triangles and circles* also coming into play, and that the secret was to adhere closely to these geometric forms.

If you draw a line from the golf ball *straight* to the target, this line, called the target line, is the baseline for the golf swing's geometry. This line is a constant on every golf shot, every time.

Working from this unchanging foundation, the golf club can be swung, and the golfer's body set up in such a way, to ensure the most efficient way to propel the golf ball straight toward the target.

The face of the golf club can be regarded as the barrel of a gun. If the gun is aimed at the target, and the trigger squeezed without changing the position of the barrel, the bullet will find the target.

And if the face of the golf club, *the barrel*, is aimed at the target, and if it is swung back and returned to precisely where it started from with regard to direction, then the golf ball—the bullet—will also find *its* target.

How is this accomplished? Using this basic fundamental model, the idea is to swing the golf club as if on a set track, so that it has little chance of getting off of that track—if it does, there will be a need to reroute the swing in order to get back on track.

This rerouting, or in-swing adjusting, is tricky business and will most certainly result in inconsistency. The club is

Target line—ball to target.

moving so fast that making exact adjustments of hundredths of inches is largely a matter of chance. Also, the rerouting wastes energy that could be applied to the overall force of the swing. A golf swing that requires in-swing adjustments will result in erratic ball striking and can rob the swing of speed and power.

The way that Tommy Bolt expressed it to me, and the way that Hogan had expressed it to him, is what follows.

47

For a dead straight shot: baseline/target line

1. At the setup, the feet, knees, hips, shoulders, and eye line must all be parallel to the baseline/target line.

2. At the set up, the leading edge of the clubface must be perpendicular to that line.

3. *This next step is absolutely vital.* The grip must be totally *neutral*, meaning that the palms and backs of your hands are also perpendicular to that line. (To get a sense of this, simply stretch your arms out in front of you and place your hands in the "prayer" position.)

4. Halfway into the backswing, when the hands are waist high (referred to from the face on view as the 9 o'clock position), the shaft and face of the club (or the plane of the shaft, depending on when the wrists begin to set) must be parallel to that line.

5. At the end of the backswing the shaft and face of the club must be parallel to that line.

6. Halfway into the downswing, when the hands return to waist high, the plane of the shaft and the face of the club must again be parallel to that line, even though the downswing plane is a bit shallower.

7. At impact, the palms and backs of the hands, and the bottom of the clubface, must have all returned to a neutral position, perpendicular to the target line. This photo simulates impact position to show clubface alignment. In an actual swing, there is more forward shaft lean at impact and more hip rotation.

8. Halfway to the finish, at the 3'o'clock (face on) position, the shaft and clubface are once again parallel to the baseline.

9. Additionally, at the top of the backswing, there must be a 90 degree angle between the left arm and the shaft.

Within this angle, energy is stored that will be released as the club moves into the impact area. If this angle is not present, the available energy is lessened.

These points all adhere to what Hogan referred to as the "Theory of Neutrality."

He said that if you stray away from these lines, you must adjust and work your way back to them. To do so requires precise, compensating timing, tricky business that results in inconsistency.

Also, the adjusting and compensating necessary to get back on track wastes energy and reduces the efficient use of energy, resulting in loss of power. Trying to make in-swing adjustments while the club is traveling at a very fast speed is futile. Even so, every now and then it works out, but due largely to a matter of luck. And under pressure it becomes even trickier.

The most powerful, consistent golf swings are swings that are energy efficient, swings that require the least amount of compensation or adjustment. They stay on track all the way.

That is why Hogan, weighing less than 150 pounds and standing barely 5'8", could often launch 300-yard drives using a persimmon wood driver and a soft balata golf ball.

The Neutral Grip

Hogan was adamant about the proper positioning of the hands. His classic book, *Ben Hogan's Five Lessons: The Modern Fundamentals of Golf,* starts out with the line, "Good golf begins with a good grip."

Hogan used the Vardon, or overlapping grip, where the hands are joined together by placing the right little finger over the left index finger. Some players have the right little finger *between* the left index and left middle finger.

Many modern players use the interlocking grip, in which the little finger of the right hand and the index finger of the left hand are intertwined. Throughout history there have even been tour players who have used the ten-finger grip, where all ten fingers are completely on the surface of the grip.

It really doesn't matter which style of grip you use, as long as it's completely neutral and as long as the hands function together as one unit, and as long as the pressure points[1] are where they need to be.

The hands are placed on the club in a neutral position, palms facing each other and perpendicular to the intended line of flight. It is important to hold the club in the left hand in such a way that the pad at the bottom of the left hand rests on top of the grip end of the club, but *not* at the very end of the grip of the club. The left thumb should be straight down the middle of the grip or very slightly to the right of center. This is the neutral position. The neutral grip, especially if you presently have a very strong grip (meaning that the hands are turned quite a bit to the right on the grip) may take a little getting used to, but it's well worth the patience to stick with it.

---

1. Read more about the pressure points in the "right thumb" section.

When making a grip change, it's a good idea to practice taking your grip with a club but without a ball as much and as often as you can. This helps you to get comfortable with the new positioning of your hands without the pressure of worrying about the ball or having to hit a shot with your new grip.

You have to be patient when making a grip change. Your shots may not be very good right away, but will improve when you adjust and feel comfortable. It will feel very uncomfortable at first but I promise you that if you stick with it and persist without reverting to your old grip, you will soon be hitting the ball with more authority, more confidence, and more control than you've ever experienced.

Here's why Hogan insisted on the neutral grip, and this will lead into the second aspect of Hogan's two-part secret:

A neutral grip maintains the integrity of the neutral aspects of the entire setup, and eliminates the need for compensatory adjustments needed to adhere to the parallel lines.

The whole idea is to stick as closely as possible to those lines throughout the entire swing. This makes the swing not only energy efficient (again, to stray from the lines and adjust to get back to them wastes energy), but increases the likelihood of returning the clubhead back to the ball squarely at impact and along the target line—the secret of accuracy.

Tiger Woods, in 2000, was swinging the club with very high efficiency. He was really on track with his swing as it adhered almost totally to the lines. His swing then required almost zero compensation. Why he would change that swing remains a mystery. He said that he was trying to make it better. I wonder if he knew that technically it couldn't get any better.

Golf swings that stay on track and very close to the parallel lines look effortless, and they put little stress on the body. They are efficient and powerful. I believe that many of Woods' physical problems are a result of his ill-advised swing changes. Look at his swing now. It hardly looks effortless. All of the dipping and lurching that he does now are attempts to get the club on track. I wonder if he even knows that.

Lots of back problems among golfers are caused by the swing being "off track." Trying to work the club back on track results in contortions and imbalances, which stress parts of the golfer's body, most often the lower back but also potentially causing injury to the hips, shoulders, and wrists.

Poor posture can also cause back problems, and we'll address that later when we talk about the golf swing in general terms.

So Hogan figured out that the secret of accuracy as well as maximum power was rooted in simple geometry—right angles, parallel lines, triangles, circles, and 45 degree angles. The secret lies in strict adherence to these lines, from setup to finish.

THE SECOND ASPECT

IN ORDER FOR the golfer to be able to stay on track—to adhere to the lines and angles *all the way through the swing*—the second aspect of Hogan's secret must be present.

It is necessary to have *two* strong sides. If you are right-handed—right-hand and right-side dominant—you must build up your left side, especially your left hand, wrist, and forearm, to the point where you have equal dexterity and strength on *both* sides.

If you don't develop the left side, the right will take over and dominate the swing and result in a collapse of the left side when force is applied.

The right side will initiate the downswing, causing the downswing plane to leave the track, and through the hitting area the hands and clubface will over-rotate.

The left side, from shoulder to legs, must be strong enough to ward off the force applied by the right side. This achieves neutrality of the forces and keeps the clubface stable while also being powerful.

Two strong sides, rather than just one dominant side, is the key to control of the clubface as well as maximum release of power.

Hogan had Bolt, and Bolt had me, spend six months developing strength and dexterity in the left hand, wrist, and forearm by performing normal and simple everyday movements with the *left* hand: opening doors, picking up and carrying things, brushing teeth, and the like. If you start to do anything right-handed you stop, catch yourself, and do it with your left.

At first, brushing the teeth can be especially challenging and even comical. And be careful with the Q-tips!

But you'll be surprised at how fast you become much more adept at using your left. Also, when you do exercises of any kind, you need to do *twice* as many reps with the left than with the right.

All of this develops the dexterity and strength that is necessary to be able to swing the golf club without one side dominating the other, maintaining neutrality while simultaneously increasing the potential for power.

Bolt also had me take left-handed practice swings and hit chips, pitches, and wedge shots with only the left arm, in order to build up the entire left side of the golf muscles.

So in a nutshell, there you have both parts of Hogan's secret, as shared with his famous student U.S. Open Champion Tommy Bolt and shared with me through Bolt.

Briefly, a capsule summary:

1. The golf swing, in essence, is geometrical. If you know the basic, fundamental geometry you can work your way toward it and in the process continuously improve your power and accuracy through energy efficiency.

2. In order for you to be able to take full advantage of your efforts, you must increase the dexterity and strength in your nondominant side.

Once you have worked your way toward the basic geometry of the swing, you can use it as a baseline to set yourself up—in effect program yourself—to work the ball in any fashion that you wish. Without changing the motion of your swing you can hit the ball straight, or bend it left-to-right and right-to-left to any extent that you want.

For example, to play a fade you simply set up just as you would for a straight shot with two exceptions. First, you set up left of the target line to allow for the fade. Second, you open the clubface a bit. Then you make the same motion that you would make when playing a straight shot. The slightly open clubface puts a little cut spin on the ball, causing it to curve from left to right. And because you aimed left of the target line, when the ball curves left to right it is working it's way back to your target. To play a draw, you repeat the same routine but from the right side of the target line, setting up to the right of the target and closing the clubface slightly. You can experiment with varying degrees of alignment and clubface adjustment to fine-tune just how much you want the ball to curve.

WHAT HOGAN ACTUALLY DID

THROUGH THE YEARS, many teachers, players, and amateur Hogan devotees have attempted to analyze Ben Hogan's golf swing. They have dissected and theorized and speculated ad nauseam.

But.

The amateur analysts base their opinions on mere speculation, armed with limited knowledge either as a player or teacher.

The player's opinions are influenced by the tenets of their own technique and without the practical experience and knowledge gained from long term teaching.

The teachers base their opinions on years of study and practical application—through teaching—of learned swing doctrines, and each teacher has his or her own style of imparting the textbook fundamentals of the golf swing. His or her style and path of study may or may not be compatible with what Hogan knew and then actually *did* when he applied what he knew.

I am going to tell you what Hogan actually did and why he did it that way, based on the principles that Hogan himself discovered.

My theory is not a theory at all. It's based on fact. My analysis is coming from three angles:

1. I was told and shown what Hogan discovered and how he applied it to his own technique.
2. I have been a player at the highest level.
3. I have been a lifelong teacher.

Before continuing, let me share my personal golf-related credentials with you, so that you may get an idea of where I'm coming from.

I've already explained my relationship to Ben Hogan's knowledge, gained through my relationship with one of his two most trusted students, Tommy Bolt.

As a player, I played on the PGA Tour sporadically and without a great deal of success. My best official finish was a rain-shortened third-place tie in the Magnolia Classic in Hattiesburg, Mississippi. The Magnolia Classic, at the time, was played opposite the Masters and counted as an official event.

I won a couple of satellite events through the years. Those satellite tournaments were the forerunners of today's developmental, or "mini," tours.

Other highlights were winning the PGA Gulf States Section Championship, beating former Major winner (PGA

Champion) Lionel Hebert by two strokes over the 54 holes. Former Ryder Cupper Freddie Haas, whom I mentioned earlier, finished eighth in that tournament. I also won the Section stroke play and match play championships through the years.

A later highlight was playing in the U.S. Senior Open at Crooked Stick in 2009. I was a low qualifier in Jasper, Alabama, gaining the one spot out of 52 qualifiers. I missed the cut at Crooked Stick, but birdied six of the last 11 holes in the second round.

My limited success on the Tour is another story. Let's just say that several elements go into attaining high levels of success out there and talent and great ball striking are only two of those.

As a teacher, I've been teaching the game for over 50 years. I've worked with every level of golfer, from beginners to PGA Tour players. I had my own golf school, which was recognized by the PGA as a major golf school. I had three locations internationally and domestically with six PGA Professionals teaching with me.

I have also authored three previous books, one of which was once featured on the cover of the PGA's Catalogue of Books. The books are *Holographic Golf*, published by Harper Collins; *Beyond Golf*, published by Stillpoint Publishing, and *Exploring the Zone*, published by Pelican Publishing and written with my close friend James Redfield, author of the phenomenal bestseller *The Celestine Prophecy*.

I have given clinics all over the United States and abroad over the last 25 years.

My teaching method has always been to use Hogan's principles, taking into consideration every student's unique physical and mental characteristics and working him or her toward Hogan's principles as closely as possible. In this way, even though every player's swing is visually different, they all share the same ultimate goal of optimal energy efficiency and consistent accuracy.

Now let's move on to exactly what Hogan did when he played golf shots.

Every golfer is unique in his or her anatomical structure, personality, emotional makeup, and way of thinking and processing information. This is not news—every good teacher knows this.

Right off the bat, skeptics and would-be experts are going to read this and say, "Hogan did not set up with his feet, hips, knees and shoulders parallel to the target line."

Yes, he did, but *only* when he wanted to play a dead straight shot. Most of the time, Hogan played what's referred to as a "power fade." A power fade is a shot that moves slightly left to right (again, assuming a right-handed player), but without the loss of distance usually associated with a left to right shot.

Hogan could also play a "draw," a right to left curving shot, when required to. But on probably 90 percent of his full shots, he liked to move it left to right.

The way that he achieved such a high-quality power fade was by setting up in such a way as to program it at the address position.

This meant that he would close his stance slightly, and open his shoulders slightly.

The slightly open shoulder position caused his swing path to move across the target line ever so slightly (this is why, as any serious student of Hogan's swing knows, his divots were pointed slightly left of target), resulting in a very slight "cut spin" being imparted to the ball. But because of his closed stance, and the resultant shallower plane of his downswing in relation to that of his backswing, his clubface was still almost square when it made contact.

Additionally, the closed stance encouraged a dropping of the hands at the start of the downswing, to slightly inside of the backswing plane. This resulted in his clubhead moving into the ball from the inside of parallel to the target line, but his slightly open shoulder position caused the clubhead to abruptly move to the inside of parallel to the target line immediately after impact. And because his left hand and wrist were as strong as his right, there was no way that the clubhead was going to turn over through impact. It would release to square, but no further. You can see evidence of this in his follow-through by how long his right arm stayed extended. No one ever kept the right arm extended so deeply into the follow-through.

So, when you couple this technique with the incredible lag that Hogan achieved in his downswing (due to his very

69

unusual degree of flexibility in the wrist/hand area), he was able to create tremendous clubhead speed while applying a 7 o'clock to 1 o'clock spin to the ball. Hence the power fade.

The ball could not go left. Hogan never had the possibility of a two-way miss after discovering the two parts of his secret.

I have heard of only two confirmed instances in which Hogan hit severe hooks when competing in his prime, and both times the players who witnessed the rarities said that Hogan had slipped on damp turf, losing his left-side brace.

All of this is clearly visible when examining photographs of his swing and impact position.

If you want to see for yourself why the ball could not go left, just examine a photograph of Hogan at impact. What you'll see is his entire left side posted up like a steel girder, and the back of his left hand in a slight convex position and considerably ahead of the shaft.

So what Hogan was doing was canceling out the possibility of a two-way miss—and any miss at all would be minimal. And what is the one key to making this work?

His grip. His grip was completely *neutral*, made possible by its positioning AND the fact that he had equal strength and dexterity in both hands. Without these features, the swing would be capable of producing a bad miss one way or the other—left or right.

How Hogan Created Power

One of the mysteries of Ben Hogan's golf swing is how it could generate such incredible power for a man his size.

He was only about 5'8" and weighed around 145 pounds, but even with the old persimmon driver and balata golf balls, he could often hit the ball close to 300 yards.

How did he do it? We've already discussed the amazing amount of lag that he created and retained during his golf swing, but there were other contributing factors to his astounding ability to generate power.

First and foremost was the fact that his swing stayed totally on track throughout his swing. There were no in-swing adjustments, no energy-wasting compensating moves that could drain the swing of energy and hence speed.

All of his effort went directly into his club gradually accelerating from start to finish. Look at his finish, at how high his hands were and how long his right arm stayed extended all the way to the finish. The dynamic arrival at his finish was a clear indication of the speed that he achieved at and through impact.

But how? Certainly not brute strength! There were many players who were significantly taller, and outweighed him by 50 or more pounds, but who found themselves way behind him in driving distance.

There's a famous story told by George Archer about a round at the Masters when he was paired with Arnold Palmer and Hogan.

On one hole on the front nine, Archer said that Palmer hit first and hit one of those classic screaming Palmer drives that took off low and rose as it finally descended into the middle of the fairway, sending Arnie's army into a frenzy of applause.

Hogan just stared down the fairway and puffed his cigarette. Finally he took it out of his mouth and threw it violently down to the ground. Archer said that it bounced hard off of his shoe. Hogan then hit his little classic power fade down the right center of the fairway. Archer said that he hit a good, solid three wood down the middle, playing for position on the 400-yard par 4.

Archer said that as they made their way down the fairway they could see that there were two balls close together and another one *70 to 80 yards* ahead. Since Archer had hit a 3 wood, he stopped at the first two balls knowing that one had to be his. But Palmer and Hogan and their caddies just kept walking on up to the other ball. Archer said that he was wondering which of the two would have to make the embarrassing walk back to his ball.

When the two arrived at the ball Hogan just stood off to the side, staring at the green and puffing his cigarette. Palmer had to stoop down and look at the ball, and then just started back to where the first two balls were. He must have been amazed and shaken, because he had hit a good drive and Hogan had hit his way past him, and the worst thing about it was that Hogan knew it without even looking at the ball.

In the course of the many interviews that I conducted with people who knew Hogan or had played with him or observed him in action first hand, several of those instances were recounted where his "extra gear" was displayed. Hogan definitely had that extra gear, and when he wanted to he could generate tremendous clubhead speed.

Let's look at the factors that enabled him to generate that kind of power.

1. We've already covered his being "on track," and how he wasted no energy when he swung.
2. His flexibility. He was unusually flexible, especially in the wrist area, and this allowed him to hinge his wrists to a greater degree than anyone else.
3. His use of "ground force." Watch a film of his swing and notice how he compresses into the ground as he makes his transition and changes direction at the end of his backswing. He begins to compress into the ground even as his club is still moving back. This, combined with the great amount of lag (angle retention of his left arm and club shaft during the downswing) results in a tremendous build up and unleashing of speed as he springs upward from the ground into and through the impact area.
4. His swing speed. Hogan had a very fast swing speed, in direct contrast to a more languid swing like Sam Snead's graceful, syrupy tempo. Hogan's swing was quick and explosive, yet in its own way graceful due to his exquisite

balance and great arm extension. When Hogan wanted to go to his extra gear, he simply ramped up his swing speed. He could do this because of the efficiency of his technique and because he had no fear of losing control just because he swung harder. No matter how fast or how hard he swung, the club stayed on track. It just went faster as it traveled through the same positions time after time.

(Regarding swing speed, you can go to any professional tournament and watch the players practice on the range. You'll see fast swings, like Rickie Fowler, and you'll see very slow tempos, like Phil Mickelson's. But regardless of the tempo, be it fast or slow, the golf club is gradually accelerating, reaching top speed at or just after impact.)

5. Hogan had two strong sides. He had developed the same strength and dexterity in his left hand that he had in his right. Unlike most people, who have a dominant side, Hogan could use power from both.

All of these factors made Ben Hogan unique when it came to striking a golf ball. Many people have commented on how his contact with the ball made a sound that was very different from anyone else's. It was because the contact was solid and pure, and it was made with explosive speed that reached a crescendo at and just after his club reached the ball.

Heaven knows what he could have done with today's technology.

The Role of the Hands and Iron Byron

What is the role of the hands in the golf swing? This is important to understand because using the hands in the wrong way is a sure swing-wrecker.

Above all, the hands serve as a *connection* between the torso and the golf club. Simply a connecting apparatus. They must be placed on the club in a position (neutral) that encourages them to remain quiet and inactive until the club approaches the hitting area.

If they are positioned incorrectly, meaning not in a neutral position, they will be forced to manipulate the club and get into the act prematurely as they attempt to reroute the clubface back to square. When they do this they run the risk of unnecessarily opening or closing the clubface. When they remain neutral, no adjustments are required and the swing can stay on track and move with total efficiency.

The USGA, the sport's governing body, has a robotic testing machine that they call "Iron Byron."

This machine stands on "legs" and has an "arm" and a "torso" and a fitting joint at the end of its arm. A club, any club, can be attached and secured to this fitting. The robot swings back, simulating a backswing, and then down and through simulating a downswing and follow through.

Iron Byron swings the same exact way, every time, enabling equipment (balls, shafts, club head materials) to be tested with extreme accuracy.

Iron Byron has no hands, just a fitting that a golf club can be connected to. Because it has no hands, there is zero chance for the club to be manipulated during the swing.

This is what you want to strive for. You want a neutral grip, to minimize the chance for manipulation, and you want to feel that the club is connected to your body through the "fitting" that is your grip.

Neutrality Is the Key to Striking a Balance Between Forces

I've got pictures of Hogan playing dead straight shots, and everything is dead square. Hogan discovered that he could program his body at address to play any shot he wanted, all due to his neutral, equally balanced grip, in terms of position *and* strength.

Let me share one true Hogan–Bolt story that illustrates the strength and solidity of Ben Hogan's grip. This story, involving a little-known Hogan drill, relates to the above section about the USGA's testing machine.

Bolt told me this one day when we were on the practice tee at Longboat Key. And it makes for a great practice drill for pros and amateurs alike.

Bolt said that one day he and Hogan were practicing at Seminole Golf Club in Florida, Hogan's winter hangout. He said that Hogan called him over and told him to watch. Hogan was hitting 5 irons and would hit a shot, go right from the finish back to the address position without moving his hands at all, and hit another shot. He repeated this 25 times without the slightest alteration in the positioning of his hands on the club. He explained to Bolt what he was practicing and then he told him to try it. Tommy said that after the second shot his grip had changed position.

Tommy told me later that the most he, a U.S. Open Champion, ever was able to do was seven shots in a row without his grip coming apart. Hogan could do it 25 straight times.

That in itself could qualify as a secret!

Anyway, it's a great drill to use in practice and doing it a few times every time you have a practice session will really help with your control of the club and encourage you to use your big muscles instead of over-using your hands.

Let's look at Hogan's secret from a different angle. He wanted a swing that did not rely on timing. He knew that the key to this was developing a swing that was so efficient that it did not require any compensating moves—no in-swing adjustments.

At some point he realized that the secret to total, pure efficiency had to lie in an innate, unchanging physical structure. Hogan probably never took a physics course, but he was smart and would practice literally all day, every day.

So eventually he developed a golf swing that used, as a starting point, a line that connected the golf ball and the golfer's intended target. He found a swing that used that line as a foundation for a series of lines and angles that matched, geometrically, that foundational line.

He discovered that if his swing adhered as closely as possible to those lines and angles that he did not have to make any in-swing adjustments.

Hogan's Left Hand

If you look at a photo of Hogan at impact you'll see that the back of his left hand is in a slight convex position. You can see that there is no chance for the right hand to take over and overpower the left and cause a "flipping" of the clubface.

In order for the left hand to be able to achieve this convex position at impact, it has to be strong enough to ward off the release of the right hand. If the left hand is significantly weaker than the right, it will be overtaken by the right hand and collapse to a concave position. This results in an increase of loft of the club face and also in a premature bottoming out of it, causing the club to contact the ground behind the ball. Also, if the grip is too strong (both hands turned too far to the right), the club face may close at impact resulting in a hook or pull.

Regarding the role of the hands, Hogan put it this way: "The left hand is the steering wheel, it maintains control of the club. The right hand applies the power, it's the accelerator." Because his left hand was so strong, he could apply as much force with his right as he wanted with no fear of the left being overpowered. In fact, he once remarked that he'd like to have three right hands!

Hogan's "Waggle"

Before Hogan would begin his swing, he would start the motion with a waggle. Then he would give a slight "kick-in" with his right knee, and the swing would take off into full flight.

His famous waggle has been written about extensively, and most descriptions refer to it as "previewing" the swing.

But his waggle was not previewing or rehearsing the way he wanted the swing to begin. What he was rehearsing was a *position*.

If you watch Hogan's waggle closely, you'll see that he was putting the club in a position that he wanted it to be in at that particular point in the swing.

When his swing would actually begin, his wrists didn't hinge immediately into the takeaway. But when he waggled, the wrists did hinge immediately.

He wanted to have the club in a specific position at that point in the swing, to ensure that it began on track. He knew that if it was on track in the early part of his swing that it would likely stay on track.

It's true that a solid address position and a one piece takeaway is vital to the first couple of feet of the swing, and most world class players pay particular attention to this aspect of their technique.

Hogan was hugely committed to practicing positions. He would rehearse swing positions in front of mirrors, windows, in hotel rooms and clubhouse locker rooms. He was drilling in the swing geometry that he had discovered and that he knew was the key to consistently controlling golf shots.

He knew that with the combination of his neutral grip and his adherence to the unchanging basic geometry of the swing that he could place his shots with great accuracy and great consistency.

His waggle was the first milepost along the way, and it set him on track right from the start.

You should follow Hogan's lead and incorporate some type of kick-start into your technique. It's important to keep the motion flowing as you prepare to swing. Starting from a frozen, dead-still position increases muscle tension, and tension is a very bad influence on rhythm and tempo.

Brandel Chamblee, in his book *The Anatomy of Greatness*, correctly points out that many of history's top players started their swing with a kicking in of the right knee. Some did it more obviously than others, like Gary Player, and others more subtly. But there's never been a great player who started the swing from a dead-still, frozen position. That invites tension and disrupts flow.

I think that Brandel did a great job with his book, pointing out the commonalities in the swings of the best players in history, but I wish that he had included *balance*.

Balance, to me, is next to the grip and address position in importance when it comes to swinging a golf club with control and power.

Every great player had the balance of a ballet dancer when they swung. Balance at address is necessary because you can't swing with balance if you don't start from a balanced position. And balance while you swing is absolutely vital for control and maximum power.

Balance at address and at the finish is *static* balance. And balance while in motion (while swinging) is *dynamic* balance.

You must have both. You can go to any driving range in the world and see golfers swinging as hard as they can, losing their footing and connection to the ground, getting off balance and losing power.

Then you can go to a PGA Tour event and watch the effortless-looking swings of world-class players driving the ball 300-plus yards. The difference is balance, which increases efficiency, which increases speed, which increases power.

Paradoxically, you have to *give up* the effort for power, which helps you to stay grounded and balanced in order to *get* it.

That's why when you watch big-time tournament golf and the pressure is ratcheted up coming down the stretch you'll see the seasoned veterans maintain their tempo and those new to contention tense up, quicken their swings, and hit wild shots. A Tour veteran who has been there many times has developed the ability to stay even-keeled, even under the stress of being in contention on the back nine on Sunday.

The waggle helps to maintain a constant but unhurried pace to the preshot routine and also helps to release tension, especially in the wrists and hands, where tension tends to start when nerves kick in.

From the time you start your preshot routine there should be uninterrupted motion that continues all the way until the swing begins. I call it "dancing through the shot," because the golf swing is definitely an athletic motion that functions best when there is graceful rhythm and great balance.

Graceful rhythm and balance are where the power comes from, not muscle tension and brute force. How many times have you watched a world-class professional hit a 300-yard drive and commented on how "effortless" the swing appeared? It's because the power was produced by three things: swing efficiency (meaning staying on track with minimal or no in-swing adjustments), great rhythm, and great balance.

One tip here for playing shots into a strong wind: do not swing harder than usual just because you're playing into a stiff breeze. Two bad things will happen: one, you'll probably get off balance and hit a wild or weak shot, and two, the ball will go much higher than usual and fall far short of its normal distance. Just stay within yourself, stay balanced, and focus on solid contact.

THE GOLF SWING
IN GENERAL

I'D LIKE TO go over the golf swing in general, incorporating the principles that Hogan espoused and including some of the other things that he did that set him apart from the other great players.

Aside from the right angles and parallel lines that make up the geometry of the swing, there are other geometrical features involved, such as circles, 45 degree angles, and triangles.

For example, the clubhead swings around and up and then back down and around again, describing a circular path called the arc.

The hips turn around and back in a half circle. At address and a few feet into the takeaway, the arms and shoulders form a triangle. At address, the club shaft should be at a 45 degree angle to the ground.

And at the top of the backswing, the club shaft and left arm should, ideally, form a 90 degree angle between them. Even at the finish, which is an indication of what transpired during the swing, the shaft of the club should ideally be close to a 45 degree angle to the ground.

Again, if you adhere to all of the lines and angles, you are operating at maximum efficiency, because you will have no need to make any in-swing adjustments. You will have stayed on track.

The Motion of the Swing

Apart from the address position and the finish, and a brief but definite "stop" at the point of change of direction, there is motion between these angles and lines. The golf swing is both static and dynamic. But if the correct motion stays "on track", the club face will return to the ball squarely and moving along the target line with great force.

Let's go through a complete perfect swing from start to finish so that you will have a clear idea of what to practice. We'll do this step-by-step. The beauty of mathematics is that no matter who you are or what you look like, 2 plus 2 will always equal 4. Likewise, if you strictly follow the baseline geometry of the golf swing and perform the motion correctly, you will hit quality golf shots. And as far as performing the correct motion is concerned, the beauty of what Hogan discovered is that by adhering to the math of the swing, the motion becomes much easier to perform!

The Setup

At address, the feet, knees, hips, and shoulders should all be parallel to the target line (the line from the ball to the target). The bottom edge of the clubface should be at a right angle (perpendicular) to the target line. The grip should be absolutely neutral, with the palms facing each other and at right angles to the target line. The left thumb sits on top of the grip, straight down the middle of the grip or very slightly to the right, and the hands are joined closely together by employing either the Vardon overlapping grip or the interlocking grip.

Generally, the stance should be about the width of the shoulders (outsides of shoulders even with the insides of feet). The weight should be evenly distributed with a balanced, athletic feeling and the knees should be slightly flexed.

There should be a slight bend at the waist to reach the ball without disturbing balance. The buttocks should stick out enough to counterbalance the forward lean. The eye line should be parallel to the target line.

The arms and shoulders should form a triangle at address, with no tension in the arms or hands but with the left arm a bit firmer than the right. The player is set and ready to begin the motion of the swing.

The Backswing

Most good players, and Hogan especially, started the swing with some kind of trigger. Sometimes called a forward press, it can be something like a slight pressing inward of the right knee or a slight pressing forward with the hands. You can clearly see these "trigger" mechanisms in any video of a good player.

This initiating movement sets the swing in motion and is the first step in the dance of the swing. I call it a dance because it's a rhythmic motion performed with balance, grace, and timing.

The club moves back by moving the triangle of shoulders and arms away from the ball until the hands reach waist high, keeping that triangle intact. This means that the hands are passive up to that point. The hips are turning away from the target (turning, not swaying laterally) until they have turned 45 degrees. The turning of the shoulders and hips have caused the weight to shift from evenly distributed to mostly on the right leg, specifically to the inside of the solidly braced right leg.

At this point, the shaft of the club should be parallel to the target line. If it is, the club is on track. As the shoulders continue to turn (actually it's a combination turn/tilt), the right arm begins to fold as the wrists continue to hinge. The left arm remains straight and firm. The shoulders turn until they have turned 90 degrees and the back faces the target. The right elbow points to the ground. At this top of the backswing position, the shaft of the club is parallel to the target line.

Also at the top, between the shaft of the club and the left arm, a 90 degree angle has been achieved due to the hinging of the wrists. Within this angle all of the power needed is stored.

The Downswing

During the backswing, the weight has shifted to the right leg, and now must be shifted back to the left as the club is brought back to the ball. This is accomplished by bumping the hips laterally very slightly.

This gets the weight started back to the left and also causes the shoulders/arms/hands/club apparatus to drop straight down, into what is commonly referred to as "the slot." This bump also serves to preserve that 90 degree angle between the shaft of the club and the left arm as the downswing progresses.

Preserving this angle is critical in two ways: first, energy is stored in this angle and the longer it's preserved, the greater the potential for clubhead speed as the club moves into the ball. Secondly, if the angle is allowed to open or increase the club will move outside of the "track."

When the hands reach waist high in the downswing, the shaft should be on a vertical plane (pointing to the sky) parallel to the target line and the right angle between the shaft and left arm still intact.

Now the hips are turning hard, the legs are driving toward the target, and the energy stored in the angle is ready to be released.

This is where it gets interesting.

As the hands begin to release the club into the ball and the angle between the left arm and shaft of the club is increased, the left hand, wrist, and forearm must be strong enough to withstand the force applied by the right hand, wrist, and arm.

If it's not, and here's the key, the club will over-rotate if the swing is on track. This is why the second aspect of Hogan's secret is so vital. It's a two-part thing, and unless both parts are there it can't work. But if both aspects are there, then the clubface has to release to square.

Here's what Tommy Bolt said to me that day on the Longboat Key practice tee when he entrusted me with Hogan's discovery: "Larry, Ben said, and these are his exact words, 'Tommy, I'm going to tell you what I've found, and I'd appreciate it if you'd keep it private for now, because I'm still competing.'"

"If you keep your swing on track by adhering as closely as you can to the lines and angles I've shown you, and if you do it with two equally strong sides, your swing will be as accurate and powerful as possible, and you will be incredibly consistent. Your swing will not rely on timing nor will it depend on hit-or-miss compensations. It will be mechanically sound."

And that is what Hogan was after—a swing that didn't have to be dependent on the randomness of day-to-day timing. He wanted a swing that was so sound mechanically that it would repeat over and over even under the intense pressure of major championships.

And did he ever find it! No golfer has ever approached Hogan in the ball-striking department. Why? Because he had the best mechanics. He didn't have to rely on timing because he did not have to make compensations and adjustments for mechanical flaws.

Check out these quotations:

From Jack Nicklaus, in his book *The Greatest Game of All: My Life in Golf*: "During the time I have played golf, the best technician, *by far*, has been Ben Hogan. No other modern player, as I see it, has approached his control of the swing, and I wonder if any player in any era has approached his control of the golf ball. Ben has probably hit more good shots and fewer poor shots than any man in history. He is the best shotmaker I've ever seen."

And from Gary Player: "I never saw a man who could swing like Ben Hogan. Sam Snead had a great, fluid, natural swing, *but Hogan had the best mechanics*. I admire Tiger Woods and Ernie Els, but Hogan was different."

Keep in mind that these accolades are coming from two of the best players of all time, Nicklaus being arguably No. 1.

The words *technician* and *mechanics* stand out and pay homage to Hogan's mastery of the geometry of the swing.

At Impact

As the club meets the ball, the clubface returns to where it was when the swing started. The bottom edge of the clubface is perpendicular to the target line and the face of the club is looking straight down that line. The energy within the angle between the left arm and shaft has been fully released. The hands, due to the neutral grip, have not over-rotated and are also back to their starting position—palms perpendicular to the target line.

The shifted weight is now moving to the left leg and the head, the "hub" of the swing, is *not* ahead of the ball. It has remained steady throughout the swing. The left arm is straight and firm as it holds off the thrust of the right side release and the shifting of the weight. A line across the shoulders is once again parallel to the target line but the driving, turning hips are perpendicular to it.

The golf ball is compressed against the clubface and is about to rebound toward the target with great speed and pure backspin—no sidespin—due to the solid, square contact with the clubface.

Halfway through the follow-through, when the hands are waist high, the shaft of the club is again parallel to the target line.

The Finish

The finish of the golf swing puts on display all that went before.

The finish position reveals what went right and what went wrong during the swing.

At the finish position the weight should be supported by the left leg, with the right foot balanced on the very tip of the front of the right foot. This indicates a proper and complete shifting of the weight.

The chest is facing the target and the shoulders have rotated a full 180 degrees during the swing and possibly even a bit more due to the tremendous unwinding during the downswing.

Throughout the golf swing, balance is key. Trying to hit the ball too hard disturbs balance, which robs the swing of the ability to produce power. Perfect balance, however, contributes to that ability and increases potential power.

Importantly, it is good to remember that there are two kinds of balance. There is *static balance* and *dynamic balance*. Static balance, as it relates to the golf swing, means balance at the start, at the top, and at the finish. Dynamic balance means balance in the midst of action, or movement. Both are necessary in order to stay in control and develop maximum clubhead speed.

The Truth about Swing Plane

The "swing plane" might be the most misunderstood concept in golf. There are books that deal with this topic—popular books that have sold in the thousands—and countless articles in the various golf magazines that talk about the "ideal" swing plane, one or two plane swings, being "off plane," and so on.

The truth is, there is one ideal swing plane for *every* player, and that ideal swing plane is determined by these three things: first, the build, or *anatomy* of the player; second, the player's *posture;* and third, the player's *ability to match the geometry of the ideal golf swing.*

If you match those lines and angles, you are on the perfect plane for *you*. It doesn't matter what angle that swing plane is on, whether it's "flat" or "upright." Those things are determined by the aforementioned three factors.

That basic, unchanging cornerstone of the geometry, the straight line from the ball to the target, never changes. That is the baseline from which we are working. And the golfer who then matches that line with the clubhead and shaft throughout the swing will be swinging on his ideal swing plane, and assuming that he has a neutral grip he will propel the ball straight toward the target.

It's as simple as that.

Now, it's important to understand that we are using a baseline that simply assumes a perfectly straight shot. There are other considerations. The important point is that the golfer can then use this baseline to craft any type of shot simply by programming himself at the address position for the desired shot.

We've already discussed how Hogan did this to create his power fade. The setup position can change that baseline—you can use a line from the ball to wherever you want—but the geometry is the same. It doesn't matter where you point your baseline, you still make the same motion of matching your lines and angles to it.

One swing. Infinite setup positions. That is important for you to understand.

You can create any shot pattern you wish by how you program your body and your club at the address position.

How Many Swings You Need to Learn

Only one. Every full golf shot can be played with exactly the same swing, the same basic motion.

For every full shot, the body and clubface is simply programmed at the setup for the type of shot the golfer intends to play. But once the setup is complete and properly programmed, the body motion is always the same.

I might get some arguments about this, but as you read the following paragraphs you'll understand what I'm saying. First of all, a golfer's swing, once performed over a certain period of time, never changes to any significant degree.

I can see a golfer from 200 yards away, one that I haven't seen swing in 30 years but one who I knew as a junior golfer, and I'll tell you who it is. It's like a fingerprint. No two are alike, and each one timelessly unique and virtually unalterable.

Even Venturi missed the boat on this. He said, in his comments in the book *Ben Hogan: The Man Behind the Mystique* that "Hogan had all these different swings, all these different finishes."

Hogan had *one* swing. The reason that he had different-looking finishes and played fades, draws, and straight shots was because he knew how to *program* his setup for the shot he wanted.

If you understand this and know what to look for when you watch video of him, it's clearly visible. But the basic motion and major tenets of his technique never varied.

Hogan's secret of the golf swing—the concept of total neutrality—is based on a shot that goes straight and exactly in the direction that the clubface is aimed. The geometrical lines—all of them—are adhered to throughout the swing.

The beauty of this is that these lines can be used, along with altered alignments of the body and clubface, to craft shots that bend or curve one way or the other. Because fairway shapes and pin locations are rarely dead straight, it is a valuable asset to be able to curve shots to fit the situation.

At this point I want to reiterate and emphasize the importance of the second part of Hogan's secret. The non-dominant side absolutely must be strengthened to the point that it is equal to the dominant side. When I say "side," I mean the whole side, from the ground up, but especially in the arm, wrist, and hand.

Without this vital aspect, the geometry cannot be used to the utmost advantage.

Now, you might get discouraged about this, but let me alleviate your concerns. You might be thinking, *I understand the importance of this, but gee, it's gonna take me forever to develop my left side so that it's equal to my right.*

Not so. You will be amazed at how quickly you can do this. You have to realize that for all these years your left arm hasn't been immobilized! To some degree it's already developed due to performing some everyday tasks.

In the drills chapter there will be drills and exercises for developing your nondominant side, along with other drills for various aspects of the golf swing.

In just a few short weeks of diligent work you will be able to bring *two* strong sides to your golf swing, neutralizing any chance of strong side dominance—a certain swing-wrecker.

HOGAN'S SECRETS OF CONCENTRATION

HOGAN WAS AS famous for his unflappable powers of focus and concentration as he was for his sublime ball-striking ability.

His desire to win was so intense that he literally blocked out any outside influence that might disrupt his singular focus. Because his focus was so intense and narrow in scope, many pegged him as being antisocial, standoffish, or worse.

He spoke very little when competing, and not at all when in contention, especially in majors. The other players, knowing Hogan's ways, usually didn't even try to start a conversation with him.

On the rare instances when he did answer to an attempt at small talk, he would reply politely, but then would absolutely not extend the conversation. The initiator would get the message.

Part of his remarkable ability to block out outside influences was his comprehensive strategic planning.

Hogan, in practice rounds, would formulate a detailed game plan on how best to attack the golf course. No detail went unnoticed.

Because his ball striking was so remarkably accurate and consistent, he was able to plan his tee shots and approach shots to land in optimum positions.

The average Tour players back then, good as they were, couldn't possibly formulate a game plan as intricate and detailed as Hogan's, simply because they weren't *sure* where their shots would finish. Hogan was sure.

There are some humorous stories associated with Hogan's silent demeanor.

Jimmy Demaret, one of Hogan's few close friends, was a champion in his own right. He won 31 PGA Tour events and was a three-time Masters Champion.

Naturally, he was paired with Hogan rather frequently. Being good friends with Hogan, one sportswriter assumed that the two spoke while playing—more than Hogan ordinarily would.

So this sportswriter asked Demaret if Hogan spoke much to him while playing. Demaret replied, "Oh yeah, he spoke to me on every green. He said, "Jimmy, you're away."

Hogan was, at all times on the course, thinking about his game plan. He was like a world-class billiards player, always playing a shot that would set up the *next* shot.

That was his secret of concentration. He epitomized the mantra of today's sports psychologists: *Stay in the present*. The difference with Hogan was that he did it completely and relentlessly. There were no lapses in his attack of the golf course.

Hogan was so immersed in his strategy that there was no room for distractions or negative thoughts.

A clear example of this was publicized in one of those "positive thinking" classics of the 1970's: the top ten players on the PGA Tour were once asked what they were thinking when standing on the tee of a long par-4 hole with water on the left and out of bounds on the right. One by one they said things such as, "My shot pattern is left to right, so I favored the left side so that I had more margin for error." Or, "When I miss I tend to miss left, so I'd try to start my shot down the right side."

When they got to Hogan, he said: "I'm focusing on a circle, 10 yards in diameter, lying in the area where I want my drive to finish."

Not only was he thinking in detail about where he wanted his shot to end up, he was already planning his approach shot to the green.

One thing that the average golfer can do to improve his or her game and improve focus and concentration is to develop a preshot routine. The preshot routine is something that all good players have. It starts when it's your turn to play your shot. It should be short, comfortable, and *unvarying*. It should be ritualistic. It should become so ingrained that nothing can disturb it. It should have a rhythm to it, a cadence. I call it a dance, a *dance into the swing*.

The preshot routine should lead straight into the forward press or waggle, and by design there should be no static time between the preshot routine and the beginning of the swing. Staying still too long breeds tension, and tension, the off-spring of fear, is fatal to the swing. Tension destroys rhythm and turns a flowing swing into just an attempt to hit.

Scott McCarron, a longtime Tour player with seven professional wins and three top tens in majors, once told me this about his preshot routine: "I even tug at my glove the same exact number of times. It's all I ever work on, my routine."

The profundity of that statement didn't really hit me until later. Of course, the starting position, or address position, is part of the routine. So Scott was saying that his entire routine was vital to the success of the upcoming shot. The routine establishes rhythm and position, and if an error occurs with either of those, the shot will most likely be adversely affected.

With Scott, or any other top player who has played the game for many years, the mechanics of the swing are not likely to change to any measurable degree. But the rhythm and tempo can get a bit off, which disturbs balance, which alters those mechanics. Hence the extreme importance of a rhythmic, unvarying pre-shot routine. *You want to "dance" into whatever address position you need in order to play whatever shot you're planning.* You want to keep the motion going right into the swing.

I even asked McCarron what he did on those days when the club just didn't feel right in his hands, or when his takeaway felt disjointed, or when his balance or tempo was a bit shaky.

I said, "Don't you check or work on your swing mechanics then?"

He said no. "Just routine, that's what I work on. Some days you're going to be a bit off, but if you start fiddling with and changing your swing mechanics when you've already got an effective golf swing, you're going to go into an endless loop of band-aid fixes and end up screwing up your swing. If I just shot 68 yesterday and hit 15 greens in regulation, why would I doubt my swing today? What gets off is something in the routine, something in the setup. So I just work on my routine, which includes the address position. I may have a bad day today but I'll more than likely snap back to a good day tomorrow. If I mess around with my proven mechanics I could end up having a string of bad days, maybe even a prolonged slump."

So there's an important lesson there. Once you've gotten your swing on track by implementing Hogan's swing principles, spend your practice time perfecting your preshot routine, which includes programming your address position for the shot you're planning to play.

Framing the Shot

One tip about starting to build your routine: almost every professional starts from directly behind the ball looking down the intended line of flight. This serves two purposes.

First, you get a clear view of the lines, or frame of reference for the upcoming shot. You *frame* the situation.

Second, it's the starting point of your routine from which you can visualize the shot you've planned and begin the dance as you literally walk into your stance.

The only way that you're going to hit good shots consistently is if you make good swings consistently. And the way to make good swings on a consistent basis is to be consistent with your routine, which includes your address position.

What makes for a consistent, unvarying routine? It has to be ritualistic, and it has to be finely detailed. It must not only be unvarying positionwise, but the rhythm must be the same. The elapsed time of your routine should be the same every time.

So, to summarize all that—you must have a consistent, unvarying preshot routine if you want to be consistent with your swing and your shotmaking.

Many of you probably wonder why you hit much better shots on the practice tee than you do on the course when actually playing. "Taking it to the course" is a universal challenge, even at times to the world's best players.

There are two big reasons for this.

First, when you're on the practice tee, you're hitting ball after ball from pretty much the same spot.

Your lines are constant, you have an unchanging frame of reference. But when you're on the course, those lines, and your frame of reference, change with every shot.

Second, when you're playing on the course you have results that matter. You're penalized for poor shots. When practicing there is no penalty for an errant shot. You simply rake over another ball.

So here's the lesson that will help you to take your game from the practice tee to the golf course.

When Hogan practiced, he didn't just beat ball after ball at warp speed as you see most weekend golfers do. With Hogan, every shot mattered. He would visualize a particular situation on the golf course that called for a certain kind of shot. He would change positions and directions so as not to be hitting with an unchanging frame of reference, just like on the course. He would then plan and execute that shot on the practice tee as if he were playing that shot for real. For him, it *was* real.

He would sometimes take a minute, and sometimes much longer between shots when practicing. Every shot was important and carried with it penalties as well as rewards. If the shot did not come off as planned, he would repeat the process until it did.

In this way, your chances of playing as well as you practice are greatly improved.

When you just hit balls indiscriminately on the range, raking over ball after ball and slashing at them mindlessly, all you're doing is ingraining bad habits. You're perpetuating bad play.

Take the lesson from Hogan, and make your practice productive. Your ball striking, your strategic planning abilities, and your scores will improve.

Hope and Expectation

The world's top players *expect* to hit a good shot every time they swing. Everyone else *hopes* to. The difference is huge.

Hogan expected to place the ball precisely where he planned to place it—in the optimum position for the next shot.

When you *expect* to hit a good shot, no room is left for negative thoughts, no room for fear. And so you're able to swing with freedom. Fear of negative results breeds tension, and tension ruins any attempt at a fluid, efficient swing.

THE FUTURE OF
THE GOLF SWING
(AND GOLF IN GENERAL)

THE GEOMETRY OF the golf swing will never change, but people do. And equipment does, and so do the golf courses. This chapter should really be called "The Future of Golf," but we'll address both.

First of all, despite the perception of some, golf has never been more popular. If you want proof, just go to any public facility and try to get a last-minute tee time.

There is a magazine that the PGA of America puts out monthly for the approximately 27,000 PGA members. Each month, there is a page in the front of the magazine that lists, state by state, the percentage up or down of rounds played statewide. As of mid-to-late 2015, and early 2016, play was up in more than 30 states.

While it is true that playing golf is expensive, with rising costs of greens fees and equipment, the lure of the game endures.

Cameron Miller, at three years old.

With regard to the declining numbers of new course construction, that is a statistic that has historically ebbed and flowed through the decades. But at the same time that the number of new courses fluctuates, the number of people who play golf steadily and consistently increases.

If this popularity is going to continue, it will become increasingly important for manufacturers to make golf equipment affordable for young, potential new golfers. Also, golf course access must remain within the budgetary constraints of these new players.

Young men or women who are in school, or are married with children, have financial priorities that exclude the feasibility of buying golf equipment or paying exorbitant greens fees or country club dues. If the game is to remain popular, it must be affordable.

Athletes in every sport are getting bigger, faster, and stronger with each passing year. Better conditioning, better nutrition, and better coaching techniques and technologies push forward the limits of performance.

With no seeming end to human creativity, you wonder what the limits are, or—are there limits at all?

But the beauty of what Hogan discovered is that regardless of all of these changes, the simple, unchanging geometry of the golf swing is what makes it most effective. If you look at photos of the top golfers from each generation of the last 100 years at the most critical positions of the golf swing (impact and pre- and post-impact positions), you'll see that they're nearly identical.

Yes, there are many ways to get to these positions, but the *easiest* way and the most repeatable way is to get to them without having to compensate during the swing for errors made at address or during the backswing.

There is only one unchanging, underlying structure to the geometry of a perfect golf swing, and following that track is the most efficient way to perform it.

As more and more young junior golfers become trained right from the beginning to stick to the geometry, the secret of the swing, the difference between winning and losing will be dependent on how smart the player is at employing strategy.

And here again is where Ben Hogan excelled.

The golf swings of many of the top young stars on the PGA Tour already are very similar looking, as opposed to the swings you see on the Champions Tour, formerly called the Senior Tour.

These young players *never* have had a faulty swing. They were taught good fundamentals and sound swing mechanics right from the start. They never had to learn compensating moves for swing flaws because they've never had flaws.

Before the advent of video analysis and trained, competent instructors who can teach the basic fundamentals and proper swing positions, players of yesteryear had to fashion their own golf swings based on what they read or by observing and copying good players. As a result, they developed swings that were individual to them and swings that they were able to make work through endless repetitions and in-swing adjustments and compensations.

So because of that you had your Miller Barbers and your Mason Rudolphs and the more modern version—Jim Furyk. These players all had and have very unorthodox, strange-looking techniques that work—most of the time.

But when the player's timing is a bit off with these unorthodox swings, the player has a bad day of ball striking.

Even a golf swing that gets a half inch off track requires that the half inch is regained, and getting that just right is tricky, hit-or-miss business.

Here's the Swing Law: *The fewer in-swing adjustments you have to make, the more consistent will be your ball striking, and the less reliant you'll be on perfect timing.*

Additionally, most of today's young players have mental coaches who school them on techniques to maximize their thinking processes on the golf course.

Once when a reporter asked Arnold Palmer if he ever had a sports psychologist, he replied that he did and that he consulted him after every round. When the reporter asked Palmer who it was, he said that his name was Jack Daniels! That shows you the difference in how golfers train these days compared with bygone eras.

Efficient course management, as you will learn in the section of this book detailing the strategic secrets of the pros, can significantly lower a player's scores.

Two players who were head and shoulders above their peers in strategically dissecting a golf course were Ben Hogan and Jack Nicklaus, and it's no coincidence that these two are at the top of every list of the best players of all time.

When I first took my grandson Cameron to the course, when he was three years old, my purpose was just to expose him to the game generally, to let him experience the atmosphere of golf.

I had no intention of teaching him yet. His attention span, I figured, would be too short. So I just gave him a little driver given to me by my friend Andy Gutter, whose grandson Xander had outgrown it. Xander had named the little club the "Big Dog."

I just let Cam start whacking balls however he wanted to.

To my amazement, after a short time he was making a pretty good golf swing, all on his own! (See photo).

Evolution? Genes? Mimicry? I don't know. I was amazed.

The future of golf is exemplified by Cam and thousands like him, kids who are in an accelerated state of evolution thanks to the technological advances of *our* generation.

PUTTING HOGAN'S SECRET TO WORK FOR YOU

THIS CHAPTER WILL prove to be the most important one in this book for you, as it will provide a detailed plan for significantly improving your golf game.

You'll learn how to use the secrets that Hogan used to improve your technique and your scoring ability.

Understanding the Geometry of the Golf Swing

Once Hogan had discovered that the most efficient golf swing had an unchangeable basic nature rooted in geometry, he then discovered how to *use* that geometry to create any type of shot pattern that the situation called for.

Starting from neutral, Hogan could shift his body angles around to program himself at address for the desired ball flight. And then all he had to do was swing. The same unaltered swing, over and over again. His setup dictated the way that the ball would fly. High, low, right to left and left to right, in predictable degrees. His swing motion never changed. He didn't *try* to alter it. Any difference in the way it looked was simply a result of his address position.

Hogan trusted the geometry. He knew that it was absolute and unchanging.

Now that you understand the simplicity of the geometry, you can put it all to work for *your* game. I am going to tell you how.

Starting from Neutral

The first thing you must learn is how to start from a completely neutral address position. This starting point must match the inherently neutral state of the target line, which is simply a straight line that runs from the ball to the intended target (and, relevant to the golf swing, this line extends a few feet behind the ball as well).

The club must be placed behind the ball with the clubface facing directly down the target line. The club's leading edge (the bottom front edge of the clubface) must be perpendicular (at a right angle) to the target line.

Your grip must be neutral, meaning that the palms of your hands are perpendicular to the target line, with your left thumb pretty much straight down the top center of the club's grip. *Slightly* to the right of center is okay, as long as it's just slightly, and as long as your left palm remains perpendicular to the target line.

Next, your stance must be neutral, which means that a line across the front of your golf shoes is parallel to the target line. Following this theme, a line across your knees, hips, and shoulders should likewise be parallel to the target line.

The Takeaway

If you look in a mirror at your address position, you'll notice that your arms and shoulders form a triangle. As you begin your backswing with your takeaway, *the triangle must be kept intact until the shaft of the club is horizontal.* The hands at this point are approximately waist high, and have remained passive, doing nothing to disturb the triangle.

The shaft of the club at this point must be parallel to the target line.

Continuing the Backswing

As the shoulders keep turning, the club simply follows the track that it started on. The right elbow folds and the wrists hinge upward. The hips have begun to rotate back with the left knee moving back behind the ball, and the hips will continue turning until they have turned 45 degrees from their starting position. When the shoulders have turned to the point where your back is facing the direction of the target, it will have turned at least 90 degrees. The wrists have hinged to the point where the shaft of the club and the left arm form at least a 90-degree (right) angle.

Also, the shaft of the club should be parallel to the target line. If it's not, it's already off track and will have to be worked back to being on track by compensations during the swing. Again, these compensations or adjustments are hit-or-miss and the effort in making these adjustments and compensations wastes a great deal of energy that could otherwise be directed to increasing the speed of the club as it moves into and beyond impact.

Interestingly, Kris Tschetter, in her book about her student/teacher relationship with Hogan, tells a great story about something Hogan believed about clubhead speed.

Hogan believed that if the club traveled at a higher speed just after impact than it did at impact, that the ball would travel farther and straighter. He told Kris that he thought that he had read something about that somewhere. He then asked her if she could try to find anything about that concept.

It took considerable digging, but sure enough she found what Hogan was referring to in some physics book that had to do with the laws of acceleration.

Hogan was delighted for the validation and thanked her for taking the time to find it.

Along those lines, if you've ever seen a karate demonstration where the karate expert breaks a two-by-four by "chopping" downward with the edge of his hand, he's using this principle.

What the expert is actually doing is trying to break an imaginary two-by-four several inches below the real board, so that as his hand contacts the real board it is accelerating toward the imaginary one!

Hogan didn't say so, but I believe that he was suggesting using this same principle when striking a golf ball. Just picture an imaginary golf ball a few inches in front of the real one as you near impact.

Perhaps this was part of the reason Hogan could hit the ball so far despite his rather small stature. And could this be yet another, unshared part of his secret? We'll never know, but it shows the scope of Hogan's analytical and introspective mind.

Now you've reached the top of the backswing. Your hips have turned 45 degrees, your shoulders have turned 90 degrees, your weight has shifted to the inside of your right leg and right foot, and the shaft of your club is parallel to the target line. There is a 90-degree angle between the shaft of your club and your left arm. You are on track, poised and ready to deliver the clubface to the ball. Because you are on track, there will be no need for any compensations for off-track positions. No need for adjustments on the downswing.

The downswing is started by getting your weight moving back toward your left side with the left hip leading the way. It subtly "bumps" a little to the left, which gets the weight moving and also pulls the "unit" of your shoulders, arms, hands, and club downward.

As your hips continue turning back to the left, this unit continues moving downward until the shaft of the club again is parallel to the target line. If it is, then you are still perfectly on track. At this point, because the shoulders, arms, and hands have done nothing independently (they've been "pulled" to this position by the weight shift), the 90-degree angle between the club shaft and your left arm has been preserved. It is within this angle that the energy is stored, ready to be released at and beyond impact.

The hips continue driving to the left and the right leg, from the ground up, drives toward the ball. The hands finally get into the act and release the angle, slamming the club into the ball with explosive force. Because you've stayed on track thus far, the club returns to the ball from where it started, with the clubface pointing straight down the target line and the leading edge perpendicular to it.

An indication that the swing has kept the club on track is confirmed when in the follow-through and the hands are waist high, the shaft of the club is once again parallel to the target line.

Another indication is when the 45-degree angle of the shaft to the ground that is established at address is duplicated at the finish when the club shaft is behind the player's back.

Another checkpoint is the triangle of the shoulders/ arms that should be preserved until the hands are waist high on the back and forward swing.

The golf swing can be viewed as a chain reaction and also a reverse chain reaction, meaning that achieving a position anywhere in the swing is dependent on some prior position.

More about the finish: the next time you watch tournament golf on television, notice how the pros, when making their practice or *preview* swings, hold the finish position in a particular place. They know that if they achieve a certain position at the finish that the swing needed to get there had to occur. So they practice repetitions of a particular finish in order to draw out the swing needed.

Notice also how balanced they are at the finish. A valuable drill is practicing finishing in perfect balance. It adds smoothness and grace to the overall look of the golf swing and promotes controlled power.

A great example of this is Jason Dufner. He has an exquisite finish position, perfectly balanced and yet hinting at the gradual acceleration that brought him there. Other great examples are Davis Love and, of course, Ben Hogan.

Timing

When a golfer's timing is on, it means that all of the parts of his swing are synchronized to the point where he is able to return the clubface to the ball squarely and facing directly down the intended line of flight. It also means that the energy of the swing is maximized and enables the clubhead to reach maximum speed at impact.

In order for this to happen, any swing flaws that are present must be compensated for *during* the swing.

But when the compensations, the adjustments, are a just a bit off, the player's timing is said to be off.

How many times have you or someone you were playing with had a bad day and declared, "My timing is off, I just can't make my swing."

For instance, if at some point during the swing the club gets *outside* of the ideal swing plane by one inch, it must be rerouted to the inside by exactly one inch in order to get back onto the ideal plane. This kind of in-swing adjustment, as you can imagine, is tricky business. It's a hit-or-miss proposition. It guarantees inconsistency.

This compensating also robs the swing of energy. Energy is wasted on unnecessary movements.

For a golf swing to be energy efficient, it must remain on track from start to finish.

Ben Hogan, with his literally thousands of hours on the practice range, was searching for two answers. First, he was searching for a way to eliminate one side of the golf course. Hogan, as any "Hoganite" knows, was plagued by a bad tendency to hook early in his career. This tendency prevented him from becoming a consistent winner.

When a golfer has the potential for a two-way miss, the uncertainty over where the ball is going has serious negative effects on his scoring ability.

So Hogan was looking for a way to ensure that the ball could not miss left.

One of the things that has contributed to the downfall of Tiger Woods' scoring ability is that for the last several years he's had a two-way miss always lurking.

The second thing that Hogan was striving for was a golf swing that did not depend on timing. He wanted a swing that was so *mechanically* sound that there was no dependency on timing—that there would be no need for in-swing adjustments or compensations.

Hogan found both through deep practice, the kind of practice that takes the practitioner to the depths of technique.

And in the depths is where the root of technique lies. You can't just hit 50 or 100 balls and discover very much.

Proof of the validity of Hogan's discoveries is in his ball striking—in his unprecedented control of the golf ball.

Another manifestation of his mastery is a fact that makes him unique among the top players in the long history of the game. Hogan never had "off" days in regard to his ball striking.

He never had bad timing days because his swing did not rely on timing. There was no need for in-swing adjustments or compensations, because his technique was rooted in the unchanging laws of physics.

How Hogan Practiced

Before I give you some drills that will help you refine your golf swing, I want to tell you about some of the important things that Hogan worked on and how he worked on them.

It is well documented that Hogan practiced a lot in front of mirrors. This kind of practice affords you the only opportunity to watch yourself as you swing. More importantly, you can *see* the positions that you're in at various points of your swing, instead of just *feeling* them.

In Hogan's day, there were lots of long hours of downtime in motel rooms, and Hogan, being the insatiable searcher for the perfect swing, took advantage of those long hours by practicing his swing positions in front of mirrors and by practicing his putting stroke on motel room carpets.

Tommy Bolt told me that Hogan took more practice swings in motel rooms and locker rooms than he ever did on driving ranges, and that's saying a lot.

His constant repetitions grooved his swing to the point that it hardly ever varied. It was just about as automatic as is humanly possible.

But repetitions are worthless if they're not correct repetitions. Otherwise you're grooving a swing that is flawed, and unless you're supremely talented and develop, through endless practice, consistent compensations and adjustments, you'll never play good golf with any semblance of consistency. You'll be caught in an endless loop of quick fixes that never last.

So what was Hogan practicing in front of those mirrors in those cheap, stark motel rooms and in locker rooms across the country?

Bolt said that he would see Hogan performing this kind of practice all the time. He said that Hogan could hardly pass by a mirror or large window without stopping, setting up as if to hit a shot, and checking some *position* of his swing.

Tommy said that he would learn much later exactly what Hogan was so intent on practicing and constantly checking.

He was checking to see if he was matching the baseline geometry of the golf swing, which he had discovered through his extensive, deep practice and his own sharp ingenuity. His analytical mind, along with his devotion to experimentation through constant repetitions on the practice range led him to discover that there was one unchanging basic model, based on physics, for swinging a golf club and hitting a golf ball most efficiently.

At the risk of being redundant, I want to repeat in different words the heart of the first part of Hogan's secret. I am doing so because it is vitally important that you come away with a thorough understanding of what Ben Hogan discovered. Once you really resonate with his baseline model, you will speed up its implementation into your own golf swing.

The Baseline Geometric Model

This baseline geometry, this model, consists of geometric figures: parallel lines, perpendicular lines (or right angles), acute (or 45-degree) angles, circles, and triangles.

By adhering to the correct positioning of these geometric figures, the golf club, via the golf swing, stays on track.

And again, if you stray away from these baseline positions, you will have to work your way back to them to get the club back on track. This will require adjustments and compensations during the swing while the club is traveling at a very high speed. Only perfect timing, along with luck, will get the club back on track. You can understand why ball striking can be inconsistent.

The world's best players get "off" now and then because their adjustments are sometimes a bit off despite the fact that they are swinging a golf club a large percentage of the time.

The average golfer, who might swing one or at best two days a week, has little chance of consistently making these complicated adjustments.

In Sum:

Ben Hogan's ball striking was the same day to day. He practically never had a bad day tee to green. His ball striking was the most consistent and controlled of any player in the long history of the game. Why? Because of the first part of his secret, the golf swing's baseline geometry, and his understanding and command of adhering to it and using it to shape shots in any way that he wanted.

HOGAN'S SECRETS OF COURSE MANAGEMENT

IMPLEMENTING THIS SECTION is a guaranteed way to lower your scores even if you ignore the rest of this book. Every player, from rank beginner to touring pro, wastes strokes by making poor decisions on the course during play or by poor planning.

This area of the game, aside from his mastery of controlling the golf ball, was a great strength of Ben Hogan's.

Like Jack Nicklaus, Hogan won many tournaments with his mind.

Millions of golfers around the world are constantly trying to improve their games by beating balls on the driving range, taking lessons, and buying the latest equipment. For many, it's a fruitless endeavor.

Fortunately, there is an easier, much more effective and quicker way to slice a significant number of strokes off of their scores.

It's called *course management*, and it is something that is easy to learn and easy to use, regardless of experience or athletic ability.

Course management involves carefully analyzing the layout of a golf course, taking into consideration things like terrain, natural and architectural hazards, types of grass, soil conditions, and subtle and not-so-subtle nuances and illusions created by course designers and course architects. Weather conditions also affect play and factor greatly day to day when planning a round.

Once armed with this easily accessible information, the golfer can devise a plan—a strategy—for playing the course most effectively.

The best players in the world move around the golf course like a chess master or billiards expert, placing each shot in optimum position. They always think one shot ahead when it comes to shot placement, with the goal of making the *next* shot easier.

Effective course management not only maximizes your scoring ability, it also enhances your enjoyment of the round, knowing that your systematic planning and execution have paid off.

Your ball striking will also benefit, because your attention to adhering to your game plan keeps you focused and in the present at all times. And the beauty of it is that whether you are a novice golfer or a PGA Tour professional, the method is the same.

In this short but valuable chapter, you will learn how to analyze and chart a golf course the way that Ben Hogan did, and how to go about devising a plan for dissecting it with surgical precision.

If you carefully study this section, and introduce its concepts into your golf game, I promise that you will cut lots of strokes off of your present average score and greatly increase your enjoyment of the game.

Mapping the Course

Golf course designers and architects create courses with several factors in mind. The course must be aesthetically pleasing. It must present challenges to the golfer. Also, environmental issues are taken into consideration—things such as drainage, effects on surrounding areas, and effects on the habitat of wildlife. Chemical usage on golf courses is carefully monitored by government agencies to ensure human and wildlife safety.

With regard to creating challenges to players, the designers try to offer several options for level of difficulty by having as many as five or six different teeing areas, affording the player his or her choice of the length of course they wish to play.

But regardless of the length of a particular hole, the designer must utilize mounds, sand bunkers, creeks, and ponds, and place them strategically so that even a shortened hole is made interesting and presents a degree of challenge. Great examples of this, even for world-class professionals, are the 100-yard par threes and 300-yard par fours that you often see in major tournaments such as the U.S. Open.

The great designers are master illusionists, and fool the golfer by creating visuals that confuse the player. Subtle ridges in greens, subtle mounds and elevation changes, and greens that tilt against the natural slope of the surrounding terrain are just a few examples.

Also, sand bunkers that by their shape and position change the golfer's perception of distance are a popular tool of crafty course designers.

Another favorite trick is to try to make the hole appear more difficult when viewed from the teeing area, and this brings us to the first step in learning how to map a course.

But first, there is a vital preliminary that must be attended to. Before you can begin to map a course and formulate a game plan, you have to determine exactly how far you typically hit your clubs—all of your clubs, excluding, of course, your putter. I say typically because slight allowances must be made for weather conditions and course conditions.

To determine these distances, choose a clear, windless day with normal humidity and moderate temperatures. Find a flat area of ground that is long enough to accommodate distances up to driver length.

You will need four things besides your set of clubs: a friend to assist you, an accurate laser rangefinder, 15 golf balls (the brand that you play with), and a pen and small notebook to record your data.

Begin with your shortest wedge and work your way upward through the entire set, hitting 15 balls with each club, aiming at the same specific target with each shot.

Strike each shot as you would normally while playing, not trying to press for extra length.

After each fifteen balls, walk out and remove the five shortest balls and the five longest.

Then choose the *middle* of the five remaining balls and stand there while your assistant stands on the spot from which you were hitting and uses the rangefinder to shoot the distance to you.

That distance is your *average* length for that club, which you then record in your notebook.

You can then always use that distance as your baseline for calculating club selection when playing.

Using that average distance as your starting point, you can then make adjustments for the conditions of the day relating to the weather and the course. We'll go into more detail regarding those conditions as we move further along.

It is also helpful to write down the *maximum* distances of each club, another aid when it comes to club selection.

Walk the Course Backward

Course architects and designers like to try to create illusions when you stand on the teeing area and look at the layout of the hole. They try to bait you into playing shots that end up in poor position.

The famous designer Pete Dye, who has designed some of the world's best golf courses, is a master at creating these illusions when you view the hole from the teeing area.

But if you walk past the green and look back toward the tee, you get a much better perspective as to how much "safe area" there actually is that you have to work with. Plus, you get great view of where the optimum landing areas are.

Walking the course backward is something that Hogan did every time he prepared for a tournament, and it was the first thing he did when he arrived at the site.

It is well worth your while to walk your home course backward, making notes of where the most desirable landing spots are. This will not only tell you what kind of shot you need to play from the tee, but it will give you a lot more confidence as you prepare to play your tee shot.

You should definitely do this on any course that you are going to play in competition, particularly one that you've never played before.

Once you have charted the course and determined your target areas, you then need to shoot distances with your rangefinder to figure out which clubs you'll need to use in order to end up comfortably within those safe areas.[2]

Walking the course backward and making notes of the safe areas are vital aspects of course management, and it's something that separated Hogan from the rest. He always said that in order to outplay your opponents, you had to also outwork them.

---

2. Note: if you aim for the *middle* of a safe area, it gives you some margin for error and increases your chances of avoiding trouble spots.

Shot Selection and Using the Terrain

Next we'll discuss playing tee shots. Once you know where the optimum landing areas are, and which clubs will send the ball safely into them, the next step is shot selection.

If there is trouble on the hole in the form of out-of-bounds stakes, fairway bunkers, or water hazards, you always want to play a shot that virtually takes the trouble out of play. For example, if there is a fairway bunker on the right side of the fairway, and your safe landing area is dead center of the fairway, you want to shift your landing area a little to the left.

What you're trying to do is play the percentages. Out-of-bounds, water hazards, and deep fairway bunkers usually lead to double bogeys or worse, and double bogeys and worse are what wreck scores.

One of the secrets of scoring is limiting mistakes to bogeys.

When planning your tee shot, you must consider the terrain. The top professionals *use* the terrain to their advantage; they "play the lay of the land."

If you're facing a dogleg left with a fairway that slopes left to right, you want to play a right-to-left shot, a draw, to the right side of the fairway so that the ball doesn't run out through the fairway. The draw into the left-to-right sloping fairway "kills" the runout, while a fade or even a straight shot will run *with* the slope and possibly through the fairway and into trouble.

So, once you know the distance you want to hit the ball, and have chosen the appropriate club, consider what the ball is going to do when it lands—which way it is likely to bounce and roll.

The Value of "Pin High"

One big, understated difference between professionals and the average or even good amateurs is the fact that professionals hit a very high percentage of their approach shots pin high or close to it, while the amateurs come up a club or more short most of the time.

This difference can account for as many as 8 to 10 strokes per round in scoring.

One reason for this is that most amateurs overestimate how far they hit their clubs, and another reason is that the professionals hit their shots more consistently solidly. Pros know that most greens are just a bit elevated, many times very subtly and cleverly disguised by the designer, and though the distance may measure 150 yards the shot actually plays closer to 160. Next time you play, keep stats on how many times your approach shot comes up short and you'll be surprised at the high percentage. It can add up to several strokes per round that could be saved simply by taking a half to a full club more on your approach shots.

A Valuable Practice Drill

Before we go on, there is a practice drill that will enhance your ability to manage your game and give your game a greater repertoire of shots.

It's a drill that Tiger Woods practiced religiously during his greatest years.

It's called the "Nine Shots Drill," and here's how it works:

With every club in your bag, except of course the putter, you practice hitting low-, medium-, and high-trajectory draws, straight shots, and fades. With each club you're hitting nine different shots.

Example: with a 5 iron, you're practicing hitting low-trajectory right-to-left draws, medium-trajectory right-to-left draws, and high trajectory right-to-left draws. And you do the same thing hitting straight shots and fades.

The beauty of this drill is that the more you do it, the better you get at it, and your confidence soars as you become more and more able to shape your shots on command to fit any shot requirement. It increases your ability to manage your game and place your shots more strategically.

It's important to remember that you have to program your setup for the type of shot you intend to play. But—just like computers—gibberish in, gibberish out. You can't hit a fade if you're set up for a hook.

Some of Hogan's Strategy

As we've said, no one has ever been better at strategy and course management than Ben Hogan. He was a tactician like no other, and he won more tournaments with his head than with spectacular shots, even though he certainly excelled in that department too.

Here are some of his maxims:

Shape your shots away from trouble
To a front pin, come in high
To a back pin, come in low
To a front pin, use a half club more
To a back pin, use a half club less
At all costs, never short-side yourself
When in trouble, your first priority is to get out of
    trouble
Don't try shots you haven't practiced

The important thing is to not deviate from these strategies, even when the results don't work out. But sticking to your strategy and persevering will save you lots of strokes on a consistent basis.

Consider the Elements

The playing conditions with regard to weather can have significant effects on golf shots. For example, if you're playing in a steady 20 mph wind, your club selection can differ by four clubs. With that wind behind you, the shot can play two clubs less than with no wind. But into that same wind you probably will need to add two clubs.

If that 20 mph wind is blowing across your target line, the wind could either help or hurt your shot, depending on the direction it's coming from and the shape of the shot you're playing.

For example, if the wind is blowing from left to right (and you're a right-hander), and you're playing a fade, the wind will help your shot as the ball will "ride" the wind.

But if you're playing a draw, the ball will be working into the crosswind, fighting it, and it won't fly as far as it would with no wind.

If you're playing on a very humid day, the way it often is in the Deep South in the summer, the ball won't travel as far as it would in low humidity. The heavy air decreases the ball's air time. Rainy conditions also decrease a golf ball's air time.

In cold temperatures the ball won't fly as far, because the ball is harder and won't compress against the club face as much as it normally would.

If you've ever played in high altitudes, such as in Denver or Mexico City, you know that the ball goes farther, often two clubs farther than it does at sea level.

All of those things must be taken into consideration when planning strategy, as 3 to 5 strokes per round can be saved just by adjusting for the conditions of the day.

Knowing When to Take Risks

Many times you're faced with a risk/reward situation when playing, and sometimes the temptation to take a chance is inviting. But that's when you have to check your ego and take a hard look at the percentages. You should never try a risky shot that you've never practiced, and never when your swing is a bit off.

But if you've hit the shot successfully in the past and you've practiced it enough to have confidence in your ability to repeat it, and, most important, if you're swinging well that day, the percentages could be in your favor.

Most of the time, however, you'll score better in the long run if you make sure that you take double bogey or worse completely out of the equation.

The biggest factor in the average player's failure to score decently is when big numbers—double bogey and worse—appear on the scorecard.

The greatest players in the world know how to score, and they know that with every shot they play their main objective is to play a shot that leaves them in a position in which the next shot is as easy as possible. Great players seldom make worse than bogey.

Never Get "Short-Sided"

When you get short-sided, it means that you've missed the green on the same side that the hole is cut on. It means that you have very little green to work with for your chip shot or pitch shot.

Usually, it will also be downhill to the hole from the edge of the green that you're playing toward. When you short-side yourself, you'll have almost no chance to get your chip or pitch shot close to the hole, and many times you'll have a very tough time making even a bogey on the hole.

Ben Hogan had a personal cardinal rule that he would, at all costs, avoid short-siding himself. He knew that avoiding double bogeys and worse would greatly increase his chances for low scores and winning tournaments.

Getting short-sided is usually the result of poor shot planning rather than a mechanical mistake, because if you plan the shot correctly, and minimize the short-side possibility, even most mechanical errors won't result in a short-side situation.

Most of the time this mistake occurs when the player just mindlessly goes for the flag.

Consider this: the pin is on the right side of the green and you aim for the green center and play a slight left-to-right fade. If you hit the shot well with the correct club selection, you'll be putting for a birdie. If you push the shot a bit, you'll be even closer to the hole.

If you pull the shot a bit, you'll still be on most greens or at least on or near the fringe for an easy chip shot.

But…if you aim straight for the flag and push the shot just a little you'll be short-sided, and you'll end up with a good chance for making a double bogey and at best a bogey.

Why would you even bring that possibility into the equation?

Playing the percentages was a huge part of Hogan's philosophy, not only on the golf course but in all aspects of his life. He carefully weighed all aspects of a situation, all possibilities, before deciding on a course of action, whether planning a golf shot or engaging in conversation. He was the ultimate thinker, calculating carefully his every decision.

To get a real sense of that, read Tim Scott's book, *Ben Hogan*. Scott worked at the Ben Hogan Company for thirteen years, eight of those as vice president of sales and marketing, and he worked closely with Hogan on a daily basis, affording him an inside view of the way that Hogan conducted himself in various areas of business, golf, and life in general.

For any Hogan fan, the book is a must-read.

Play smart, play the percentages, and you'll increase your chances of avoiding big numbers and you'll see your handicap plummet!

"Working" the Ball

"Working" the ball means curving it left to right (fading it) or right to left (drawing it).

Some might ask why Hogan, if he knew the secret to hitting straight shots every time, would purposely work the ball one way or the other on most shots.

The answer is simple. Hogan figured out that if he aimed straight for the target, and attempted to hit a straight shot directly at it, that *any* deviation whatsoever, however slight, would have the ball working *away* from the target.

However, he knew that if he tried to work the ball toward the target that the curving ball would be always moving closer and closer to it. Again, playing percentages.

For example, if the hole was cut on the right side of the green, Hogan would aim for the center of the green and play a left-to-right fade, or cut shot, as the pros call it.

That way, if the ball stayed straight he would be on the green with a makeable birdie putt and a sure par, and if it did fade, it would be moving toward the hole all the way.

Hogan could move the ball either way or hit it straight, but he favored the fade on most shots because a fade will stop more quickly when it lands on the ground. He had total control of the ball, and could trust that it would do exactly as he planned.

Tommy Bolt said that just about every time Hogan played a dead-straight shot it was from about 120 yards in, and he would set up accordingly.

If you look at video footage of Hogan playing in competition, you'll see that on those shorter shots his setup was square, as opposed to his closed-stance, open-shoulder setup when playing his stock shot—the power fade.

The ability to work the ball is a valuable asset for maximizing course management skills, and it's why the "nine shot" drill is an important one to practice.

One more tip on course management, and this one involves putting: always play just a little more break than you think you need, and try to always reach the hole.

Most amateurs miss the overwhelming majority of their putts on the low side, while the percentage of low-side misses by professionals is much lower. Also, the pros are rarely short on their putts, while amateurs typically miss on the low side of the hole and short.

Hopefully these course management tips will help to significantly lower your average score. Most amateurs hit a number of good golf shots during the course of a round, but fail to capitalize on them because of a lack of efficient planning. By going about your round in a planned, systematic way, you can avoid many stroke wasting errors.

Remember, aiming at the *middle* of safe areas greatly increases your chances of avoiding trouble.

The secret of scoring is how good your bad shots are, and where they end up. Proper planning is the key.

Famously, Ben Hogan, considered by Jack Nicklaus, Arnold Palmer, and most every top professional of the last six decades to be the greatest ball striker in the history of the game, said that he only hit three to five perfect shots in any round of golf.

But Hogan's "imperfect" shots were still very much in play and afforded him the opportunity to still score well. His course management skills were perhaps even superior to his legendary ball striking ability.

Just like the tortoise and the hare, you'll beat a lot of long hitters by keeping the ball in play and avoiding penalty shots.

PRACTICE DRILLS

NOW THAT YOU know the geometry of the swing, and that it is a constant, you need to know the best way to practice your way toward it. The good news is that as you work your way through the adjustments and compensations that have been stifling your progress, you can eliminate them one by one, and as you do your golf swing will become more consistent and more powerful.

This chapter will teach you special drills that will help you streamline your technique and strip away energy-draining compensations. These drills can be done on the practice tee or indoors when the weather is uncooperative.

First, I want to explain the concept of drills and how they work to improve your swing.

A drill is a golfing exercise that is intended to train a specific swing part. Drills should be done intermittently while practicing with the idea of *blending* the drill exercise into the full, flowing swing. You should not be thinking of the drill while playing a full shot, but rather let the drill repetitions eventually blend into your technique.

If you go to a PGA Tour event and watch the pros practice, you'll see them doing drill repetitions and then hitting a few shots.

For instance, you'll notice many players practicing their takeaway.

They'll take the club back a few feet and stop and check the position of the clubface and shaft. They'll keep doing the takeaway drill until it's in the position they want, and then hit a shot.

The more they do this, the more likely they are to match the drill position to the position they're in when actually hitting the shot.

One of the great things about drills is that most of them can be done anywhere that you can safely swing a golf club.

These drills can and should be performed at full speed and in slow motion. The teacher Harvey Penick, author of *The Little Red Book*, used slow-motion drills as an important aspect of his teaching philosophy. Performing a drill in slow motion ensures that the desired positions are achieved and also gives you a chance to *feel* the positions. At full speed the swing happens so fast that a lot of the feel is lost.

Also, when you perform a drill in slow motion you have a much better chance of putting the club in the correct positions. After a number of repetitions like this you begin to feel the correct positions, which greatly increases your ability to match those positions, when you swing at full speed.

Drill 1: The Mirror Image

This drill, and in fact all of the drills, is most effective when done in front of a mirror. In this one, you want to face the mirror and assume your address position. It's a chance to see yourself and mold your body into a correct starting position while visually confirming whether it's correct or not. When you're actually hitting a shot, you can't see what you're doing, so it's important to "drill it in" correctly while confirming it by what you see in the mirror. What you want is a balanced starting position. You want to see a triangle formed by your waistline, your legs, and the ground, and another formed by your shoulders and arms. Also, you want to see a neutral grip, with the backs of your hands facing directly toward and away from the target, palms facing each other and perpendicular to the target line. Your weight should be evenly distributed and not leaning forward or backward. Ideally, your eyeline should be parallel to the target line.

You want to feel firmly rooted to the ground, but there should be no tension anywhere in your body. You'll be relaxed but athletic and reflexive and ready to move with balance. Keep practicing this setup in front of the mirror until you can automatically set up the same way when you address the golf ball. You can confirm your progress by having a friend take a picture of your setup in front of the mirror and over the ball and compare them.

Remember, what you're doing at address is "programming the computer," and you've got to get it right.

"Gibberish in, gibberish out!" You don't want to set yourself up to need adjustments during the swing because of flaws in the address position.

Drill 2: The Takeaway Drill

After you've mastered putting yourself into the correct starting position, the next step is setting the club in motion on the correct track. The initial part of the motion is vital, because if it's not on track to begin with, you're going to have to get it back on track during the swing. And that's very tricky business.

From the address position, (and again, using a mirror is optimum), take the club away from the ball by moving the entire triangle formed by your shoulders and arms, keeping it intact, until the shaft of the club is waist high and parallel to the target line. As an aid in determining if you've got it right, you can lay an alignment rod or yardstick on the ground to act as the target line. If you face sideways to the mirror, you'll be able to tell if your position matches parallel to that line.

Importantly, if your grip is neutral, at this waist-high position the face of your club will be parallel to the target line with the toe of the club pointing upward.

Here is another facet to this drill that teaches you to get the feel of the way the neutral grip operates during the takeaway: without a club in your hands, start with your arms extended in front of you in the address position with your hands in the "prayer" position with your hands pressed together. Then take the triangle back until your hands are waist high. If your hands are in a neutral position the back of your left hand will be facing the target line and parallel to it. The palm of your right hand will be facing the target line and parallel to it. At this point, if you were holding a club, the toe of the club would be pointing straight up at the sky and the face of the club would be facing the target line and parallel to it.

This is a neutral position and the shaft of the club would be parallel to the target line—the baseline of the swing geometry—and you have "matched the lines." You are perfectly on track.

Performing this drill repeatedly will get you comfortable with starting your golf swing on track.[3]

Drill 3: The Top of the Backswing "Pose Drill"

First, put yourself in the waist-high position and hold it for a few seconds. Then, continue to turn your shoulders and hips back, letting your right arm begin to fold as the wrists begin to hinge while keeping the left arm extended. When your back is facing the target you have turned your shoulders 90 degrees. That is the end of your backswing. Your club shaft should be parallel to your target line, just as it was at the waist-high position. You are in a neutral, fully wound and balanced position at the top. There should be a

---

3. Performing the takeaway drill with the left arm only will quickly increase the strength and dexterity of your left hand and arm.

90-degree angle between your left arm and the shaft of the club. You are poised at the top, set, and ready to make your move toward the ball. Remember, drills need repetitions. The more reps, the faster the drill will blend into—and become an integral part of—your swing.[4]

Drill 4: Halfway Down

Assume your position at the top of your backswing, making sure that you're "on track" with the shaft parallel to the target line. Then start down with the left hip leading the weight shift, causing the shoulders/arms/hands/club unit to drop down. When the hands are waist high, stop. The shaft of your club should be vertically parallel to the target line. If it is not—if it is inside or outside of it—adjust it to match the target line and stop. Look down as if looking at the ball and feel where the club is. Doing this repeatedly will ingrain the feeling of the correct position. Again, this position is another integral part of an on-track golf swing.

Drill 5: At Impact

Facing the mirror, go slowly from your halfway-down position until your clubface reaches the ball. You'll want to actually have a ball on the ground so that you can simulate

---

4. Important note: as you make your backswing, your right knee should stay in its place. There should be absolutely no drifting to the right of your right knee. It has to offer resistance as you rotate to the top. This resistance helps to "wind the spring." If the right knee drifts, the resistance is lost and power and accuracy will be minimized.

the impact position. At impact, your hips should have continued to turn to the point where they are 45 degrees to the target line past the ball. Your head should still be in place and *not* past the ball. The clubface should be facing straight down the target line with the leading edge perpendicular to it. And both arms should be straight and extended as a result of the release of the hands, opening the angle between the left arm and the shaft and releasing the energy stored within it.

Drill 6: Halfway Through

This position is the mirror image (excuse the pun) of the halfway back position, but instead of the shaft being vertically parallel to the target line, it is simply parallel to it.[5] Both arms are still fully extended and the clubface is "chasing" the ball down the target line.

Drill 7: The Finish

The finish of the golf swing is the product of the positions and movements that preceded it. You can tell a lot about the quality of any particular swing by observing the finish position. That's why in one of my books (*Holographic Golf*), I recommended actually practicing a good finish position. Practicing the finish is something that world class players do all the time, because they know that in order to arrive at a

---

5. Halfway back and halfway through the shaft position is dependent on the degree of wrist hinge, but its plane is always parallel to the target line.

good finish, the motion and positions that came before caused it. It's that "reverse chain reaction" principle at work. At the finish, you should be balanced with your weight mainly on your left leg and with your right foot balanced on your toes. Someone standing behind you (facing down the target line) should be able to see all of the bottom of your right shoe. Your chest should be facing straight ahead, perpendicular to the target line, and your hands should be high, with your club shaft forming a 45-degree angle with the ground.

Also, if you have swung in balance, you should be able to hold that balanced finish position for at least a few seconds without teetering over.

Again, with regard to the golf swing, there are two kinds of balance: static balance and dynamic balance. Static balance is when you're perfectly balanced at address, at the end of your backswing, and at the finish. Dynamic balance is when you're balanced while in free-flowing motion. The two are equally important. When you compromise balance in any way when performing a golf swing, you're reducing your chances for a solid strike and you're greatly reducing your ability to generate power.

Make sure that you work on balance every time you practice, by making sure that you begin, at address, with a balanced, athletic feel, and finish your swing being able to hold a balanced, grounded position.

Balance is the cornerstone of power. When you swing too hard in an effort to produce more power, your balance becomes compromised and you actually reduce your ability to create clubhead speed, thereby preventing the very thing you're striving for. But when you start with static balance, and swing with dynamic balance, you're able to maximize your clubhead speed.

It makes no difference which sport or activity you're engaging in, if you're off balance, you're going to be weak and inaccurate.

Here's a great way to work on and improve your balance: first of all, balance begins with awareness of your center of gravity. Your center of gravity is about two inches above your navel. In the martial arts this is called the "one point." To be fully balanced, you can't have an excess of your weight anywhere near the extremities of your body. It would be like a skyscraper designed improperly with too much weight near the top. The building would be top-heavy.

It's the same with your body. Too much weight distributed away from your center of gravity and you'll be off balance. Evenly distributed balance gives stability.

So, being aware of your center is the first step.

Try this experiment: try standing on one leg. See how long you can stand this way before beginning to lose your balance. Probably not very long. Now stand on that same one leg while holding your middle finger on your one point.

Feel how this stabilizes your weight distribution and allows you to keep your balance much longer—until your attention wavers.

This is a great exercise to perform often as it keeps you aware of your center. Eventually you can expand the concept and apply it to your golf swing.

Here's how: at address, put your attention, your mental focus, on your one point. Let your swing begin from *there*. If you keep working on this, you'll find yourself more grounded and balanced as you swing, and you'll produce that "effortless power" that you see when you watch the pros.

There's an added benefit to becoming aware of your center. When you're able to operate from your center, you are disassociating from being in your head. When you're overthinking you're becoming victim to the "busy mind" state, and that's not good for calm, clear decision making. In addition to effectively freezing your muscles and destroying flexibility, the busy mind lets the ego take charge, and that's not good for performance. Better to have a calm, quiet mind and let the subconscious and the "smart body" take over and operate from their intelligent, stored-up experience.

If you doubt how smart the body is, think of this: how many times did you stroke a 40-foot putt and as soon as you hit it you said to yourself, *That's short, it's not going to reach the hole!* And the ball stops one or two inches short of the cup. How did you know?

Because the body could "feel" that the ball did not have the speed to reach. You've got to trust your body and its intelligence based on experience. It doesn't forget, unlike the busy mind.

Do you think an NFL quarterback, seeing a streaking wide receiver cut across the field 40 yards away, thinks about how far he has to draw his arm back to fire a pass? No; he trusts his body to know and he puts the ball right on the money.

Trust your body, focus on your center, and quiet your mind. Get the busy mind and the ego out of the way so that you can just perform what you've practiced.

About Practice

In *Beyond Golf*, my second book, I wrote about a type of practice that I termed "Deep Practice."

Ben Hogan was the first career professional player to engage in this form of practice, and it played a great part in his eventual discoveries.

Deep practice means practicing at long, uninterrupted intervals, and it allows the practitioner to reach the depths of his endeavor.

It is only at these depths that the subtleties can be touched upon, and in the case of the golf swing, felt.

Brief, superficial practice doesn't reach those depths, and the practitioner never feels the subtleties of the swing—consequently, the necessary adjustments can't be made.

The secrets of the ocean are never revealed in shallow waters, and likewise, the secrets of the golf swing are not revealed just by hitting a few balls.

Of course, engaging in deep practice requires a high level of commitment, and making that commitment is not an easy thing.

Hogan *loved* to practice. The practice tee for him was a combination of things. It was his playground, his research lab, his meditation studio, and in some ways, his cathedral. He loved hitting balls all day, every day.

It's no wonder that, given that type of dedication, along with his inquisitive mind and physical gifts, he was able to achieve the degree of mastery he displayed to the world during his years of dominance.

A great example of the cleverness and dedication that Hogan possessed can be found in a story that Bing Crosby told to his son Nathaniel, who incidentally was a great amateur player, winning, among other things, the United States Amateur championship. Bing and Hogan were friends, and along with their wives would socialize periodically.

Bing Crosby related this story to his son about one of those occasions when the families would get together:

After Hogan's horrific accident in 1949, as his recuperative efforts progressed, he began to take Valerie dancing a couple nights a week. This was very odd because Hogan did not like to dance and Valerie had always had a difficult time getting him to, even at weddings and other social gatherings.

So naturally she was delighted at this unexpected behavioral about-face! She even commented later that Ben had become quite adept at the foxtrot.

But her delight was tempered when he confided that the only reason he was doing this was to build up his legs for a planned return to competition sometime in the future.

The fact remained—he still hated to dance!

If you're serious about your golf game you should consider trying a deep practice session, just to experience how such a session can take you to a place you've never been before, a place where you'll feel the subtleties of your golf swing.

It's when you can feel the subtleties that small adjustments can be made. Golf involves a great deal of feel because we can't watch ourselves when we swing, so it's important to learn what it feels like when we hit good shots and when we hit bad shots.

If you want to try a deep practice session, you'll have to set aside at least six or seven hours on a good-weather day. If it's your first time you should do it under ideal conditions, with good grass to hit off of and real good-quality practice balls.

You should commit to hitting at least 500 to 600 balls in this time frame, of course taking short rest breaks in between. Also have a supply of cool drinking water and a few band aids, because if you're not used to hitting a lot of golf balls you're likely to develop a blister or two unless you protect your skin.

After a while you should start to be able to feel your swing in great detail, and you'll begin to feel what's going on with your body on good shots and poor ones.

This is when you'll be able to start making little changes that solidify the effective aspects of your swing and slowly erode away the faults.

Be patient, because in order to break a bad habit you have to form a new one and repeat it enough times until the new habit becomes ingrained.

If you can commit to this type of practice you have the possibility of truly transforming your golf swing, greatly increasing your enjoyment of the game, and significantly lowering your scores.

THE BEN HOGAN GOLF COMPANY

PRECISION IS BACK! That's the battle cry of the "new" Ben Hogan Golf Company. Once again in Fort Worth, Texas, the company that Hogan built has been resurrected with the same uncompromising quality that its founder demanded.

Responsible for this rebirth is Terry Koehler, president and CEO.

Terry is a former director of marketing for the Ben Hogan Golf Company, before it was sold and Hogan retired.

Eventually, Perry Ellis International obtained the rights and the golf club end of the company essentially died.

Terry, who founded a successful company specializing in custom wedges, became interested in resurrecting the Hogan company and restoring it to prominence in the industry.

Terry Koehler is a Texas native who grew up idolizing Ben Hogan. His father actually played with Hogan when Terry was young.

After extensive interviews with numerous suitors, the Perry Ellis Company selected Terry to take on the rebirth of the Hogan company.

Only into its second year, the new Ben Hogan Golf Company is being lauded by PGA Golf Professionals and the golfing population as the real deal. It's easy to see why when you look at and pick up the new Fort Worth Irons, as they are named.

Those familiar with the quality, workmanship, and performance of the classic Hogan Irons of yesteryear will instantly recognize the same characteristics.

When I first received my set (I have signed on as a Hogan Advisory Staff member), I went to the practice tee at my club with no small measure of trepidation. It's always that way when you get a new set of clubs and set out to hit them for the first time, not sure of what to expect. I put a ball down and grabbed the 42-degree iron (the new Hogan irons don't use numbered clubs, they use lofts) and after a couple of practice swings hit the first shot.

Dead straight, pure, and solid. I knew right away that they were perfect. I couldn't wait to hit the rest of them and the session continued as it began.

All I can tell you is that Ben Hogan would be exceedingly proud of what Terry Koehler has done. He has resurrected his company and instilled the very same quality that Hogan created and demanded.

Then I visited the company in Fort Worth and was impressed all over again. Top-notch facilities, top-notch people, and quality control foreign to most companies these days.

INTERESTING STORIES FROM MY 60 YEARS IN GOLF

SIXTY YEARS IS a long time, but they've gone by so fast that I can hardly believe it. They say time flies when you're having fun, and I've got to believe it because my time in golf has been fun for sure.

Of course, the nature of the game is that it will sometimes break your heart, but then so does love.

Golf has been my life. I've heard many people (even top-notch Tour players) say, "It's only a game" or "How you play is not who you are."

Not true for me. For me, my devotion to the art and science of golf has led me to be self-defined by how I practice my art.

How I perform has always been who I am, at least to me.

Golf has broken my heart many times, but it has also lifted me, at times, to great heights of utter joy, fulfillment, and satisfaction.

There was a rather humorous statement made by a former Tour player who didn't experience a lot of success in a career that lingered just a little too long.

When asked to sum up his playing career on the tour, he responded by saying that he'd retired with "an empty money clip and a pocketful of memories."

And it's true that the memories are priceless, as are the lifelong friendships and the valuable connections.

Let me tell you about the most spectacular give-and-take that the game has provided me in these 60-plus years. This story will illustrate to you the complexity of the relationship between golf and the golfer.

The 2009 United States Senior Open

First, a little background:

As soon as I turned 50, I entered qualifying school for what was then called the Senior Tour. Now it is called the Champions Tour. The Champions Tour is where the stars of the PGA Tour go when it's time to go out to pasture and get richer.

The first stage was in San Antonio, and I practiced hard leading up to it. It was a 72-hole test at Fair Oaks Golf Club, where 10 spots were up for grabs with about 110 entrants. The 10 qualifiers would then advance to the finals at Sawgrass in Ponte Vedra, Florida.

I was really well prepared as I teed off in the first round. Primed for a good start. And then I shot 76, four shots out of the top 10. I was more angry than upset, because I had felt *so* ready! Maybe too ready, too keyed up. I hadn't played relaxed. I was tight. But I knew that I was swinging well and quietly resolved to come back strong. I shot 72 in the second round and at least kept myself within striking range. The third round turned up cool and very windy, and the scores were certain to go up, but I kept up the good rhythm and confidently put together the low round of the day, a 3-under-par 69 in tough conditions. This vaulted me into the top 10, but I would have to maintain that position in the final round. There was no cushion; I would have to have a good round to stay in the top ten.

The weather improved for the final round and my swing held up as I shot a pressure-packed, steady round of 1-under-par 71, finishing fifth and earning my ticket to the finals.

The finals would be contested at Sawgrass, and the field would be made up of all of the first-stage qualifiers from the five sites, and all of the Senior Tour players who finished out of the top 31 list of money winners from the previous season, plus various other "exempt from first stage" players. So the field was about 125 players who competed over 72 holes for just eight spots. Those eight would be totally exempt on the Senior Tour for the next season.

There would be a 36-hole cut, which would reduce the field to the low 50 players after the first two rounds.

My caddy was my good friend Ken Lang, the husband of the celebrated career amateur Martha Lang, who is a member of the Alabama Sports Hall of Fame and has won just about everything there is to win in ladies' amateur golf.

Ken caddied for Martha in most of her many victories, and is the perfect person to have caddying for you in a pressure-filled situation. He is competent, calm, and even-keeled, and has a way of keeping his player relaxed and focused. Ken was a steadying influence during that first stage in San Antonio.

Well, we made the 36-hole cut by a few shots but were five or six shots out of the top eight. I battled hard and still had a chance going into the final round, but it turned up windy and cold and I needed about a 68 to make it into the top eight spots.

In those conditions, I could do no better than 75, and I just didn't make enough putts. I left somewhat dejected, but knew that I had given it my very best. Eight spots are just not enough, and a lot of very good players, players who could make a lot of money on the Tour, went home empty.

Starting the next year, I would attempt to qualify every summer for the U.S. Senior Open. These qualifyings were ridiculously difficult because they typically would have about 25 qualifying sites around the country with each site having 75 to 110 players for sometimes one, two, or three spots!

I had some really close calls. I was first alternate several times and second alternate several times, missing out twice in sudden-death playoffs for first place and medalist honors.

Then finally in 2009 at Jasper, Alabama, at Musgrove Country Club, I broke through. It was just a few months before my 62nd birthday. We had 59 players for *one* spot, and I shot 69. I played early that day and posted my score.

I came close to leaving, not thinking it possible that with all those good players still out on the course that no one would turn in a better score. But instead I went upstairs in the clubhouse to have lunch with one of the guys I'd played with. An hour later I went downstairs to look at the leaderboard before heading for home, and incredibly, I was still leading.

There were five threesomes still on the course, and the players still out there included a couple of seasoned Champion Tour players who nonetheless had to qualify for this event.

I wasn't getting my hopes up, but one by one the scores were posted, and unbelievably my 69 was holding up.

I was watching from the scoreboard area up on the balcony and the view was clear of the 18th green. In the last threesome was James Mason, a good player from Georgia who had played in many Champion Tour tournaments, and word came to us that he had to birdie the 18th hole to tie me. I thought, *Here we go again*, as he lined up about an 8-foot putt for a birdie 4.

I admit, I was holding my breath as his putt hit the hole but spun out. The USGA official in charge turned to me and said, "You've got it!"

Sort of in shock, I accepted the beautiful USGA medal and tournament information packet and walked to my car in somewhat of a daze.

When I was getting in my car, one of the players, Steve Hudson, walked up to me. Steve is a great player and has qualified for the Senior Open several times. Musgrove is his home course and he was a solid favorite to win this qualifying spot.

It must have been a bitter disappointment for him to miss out on his home course. Apparently he'd overheard me telling the USGA official that I'd been an alternate seven times and that it was really great to finally get in the big tournament.

Anyway, Steve must have sensed the emotions that I was feeling as I started to get in my car with medal in hand. He came up to me, and with touching sincerity said that he wanted to congratulate me and that he was happy for me. What a show of class. I'll never forget it. It's a perfect example of the kind of people who play the game and a tribute to the lessons that the game teaches.

If everyone on the planet played this wonderful game, we'd have no problems at all in this world. Golf teaches all of the important life lessons.

Once alone in my car as I made the 45-minute drive back to Birmingham, where we were living at the time, I will happily admit that some tears were silently shed. It had been a long, disappointing quest, and I'd finally done it.

So anyway, back to the purpose of this story, which is to illustrate the joys and sorrows of high-level competitive golf.

The 2009 U.S. Senior Open was contested at Crooked Stick Country Club, a great Pete Dye design located in Carmel, Indiana, a suburb of Indianapolis.

Obviously, it had been a very long time since I'd competed on a world-class level, and it showed. That little extra degree of tightness, that slight quickening of the breath, that busy mind racing all over the place. Cognitively, I knew how to quiet the demons, but the conscious self was too overwhelmed to allow the subconscious to perform the way it knew how.

Connie and I arrived at Crooked Stick and the first order of business was to procure a caddy, preferably a local one who was familiar with the course. I got lucky when the director of golf at the club recommended Nick Trimpe, a young college student who caddied at the club part-time. As an interesting footnote, Nick was the regular caddy for Peyton Manning, who was a member of Crooked Stick.

After meeting Nick and getting to know him, we headed to the practice tee to warm up for a practice round. I then got my first look at the course with my entourage looking on. In my gallery along with Connie were my three sons, Ryan, Jeffrey, and Jonathan; my cousin Buddy Breaux; Connie's brother, Travis; his friend, Upton; Upton's son; and my close friends Andy, Ann, and Barrett Gutter; and James Redfield.

After two days of practice and learning the course, it was showtime!

A professional golfer always starts a tournament with a feeling of optimism, even when his game is not particularly sharp. It's just the nature of the sport, that the unknown is always lurking close by—the good as well as the bad. I've played extremely well after a horrible warmup, and very poorly after a flawless practice session. It's one of the things that make golf so intriguing—the fact that every round is different and you never know what to expect.

So I was ready, or so I thought!

When I arrived at the first tee, I felt relaxed and confident, until the starter called my name. Looking around, I saw thousands of people in the stands and standing all around the first tee area.

The only way I can describe the feeling is that everything seemed *blurred*. I tried to focus on my target and on my preshot routine, all the things that I knew were the best way to combat my nerves.

And it worked, somehow. I drilled my opening tee shot straight and long, splitting the middle of the fairway on the very tight, short, par-4 opening hole. My gallery cheered.

Arriving at my ball, Nick and I figured we had, right at 105 yards, a perfect smooth pitching wedge shot. This was what we call a green-light special, as the hole was cut in the left center of the middle of the green, a very accessible location. A birdie opportunity. For me, a perfect distance for a smooth, unforced pitching wedge.

The 18th green is very close to the first hole at Crooked Stick, and apparently one of the big names was putting for birdie there as I got ready to swing. I believe it was either Greg Norman or Tom Watson, who were playing together.

Whoever it was obviously made a birdie putt, likely of considerable length, just as I reached the top of my backswing. And as my downswing started, the explosion of applause followed. The result was a flinch and an uncontrolled downswing speed. My wedge shot flew straight for the flag on this smallish green, but it flew a few yards too far and bounded over the green and into some gnarly grass some 15 yards from the flag. Instead of a short birdie putt I now had an extremely difficult pitch out of this unpredictable lie to a fast, downhill green. Not good.

This was the worst way to start a major, especially when you haven't played against world-class golfers in a long time. You want a nice, easy start with a few comfortable pars. Now I was trying to figure out how to escape with just a bogey. Plus, I was a bit rattled by what had just happened.

With the kind of lie I had in that thick, gnarly grass, you just can't predict how the ball is going to come out. One time it will shoot out with zero backspin, and the next time it will go about three feet as the grass gets between the club and ball and completely deadens the shot. This time it went three feet. Now I was not just a little rattled; I was a *lot* rattled. What should have been a great birdie opportunity now had the potential to become a disaster.

Somehow I managed to get the next one to about four feet and shakily wiggled it in for a bogey 5, but my head was swimming.

So on I went in this kind of half-stupor, which in retrospect was not solely a result of the spectacle I'd made of the first hole. It was a combination of that plus the general undercurrent of nerves that had been lurking just beneath the surface, despite my attempts to stay cool and despite the fact that in all of my practice sessions I'd struck the ball pretty well. You can fool the ego with fantasy, but when you get down to the heart of the matter, the subconscious rules. And one by one, the wheels loosened, and one by one, off they came.

The first 25 holes of this tournament produced, for me, the most humiliating and embarrassing stretch of holes in my long career in tournament golf. And right in front of my friends and family, who surely were in pain having to witness this total meltdown. I was zombielike, playing as if in shock, hitting shots that were so bad that I normally couldn't even hit those shots intentionally. After those 25 holes I was 16 over par, with several triple bogeys and a host of doubles.

But then something extraordinary happened.

On my way to the tee box of the eighth hole at Crooked Stick, which would be my 26th of the tournament, my oldest son Ryan, in an attempt to bolster my spirit, yelled out, "You're the man!" as I passed by and glanced at him behind the gallery ropes. And some drunken idiot—you know the kind—yelled out, "Yeah, he's the man—he's 16 over par"!

To which Ryan shot back, "You're damn right he's the man; he's my *dad!*"

And I swear it was like a lightning bolt shot through me. First, I felt a flood of emotion as I realized the power of a son's love for his father. And then it made me think of *my* dad, who was dying of Alzheimer's disease back in New Orleans.

My dad would have loved to have been in my gallery that day. He would have been so proud to see me competing in one of golf's majors. He started me in the game, and had given me every tool I needed to make it this far. The score would have meant nothing to him. He would pass away on October 18, just a few months after the tournament.

So I thought of him and the kind of man he was, and how he would have handled what I was going through. He would have accepted this embarrassing retreat from par with grace and dignity, holding his head up and smiling to himself at the absurdity of it all. He always had a great, and often ironic, sense of humor. I guess that after enduring the Great Depression and serving in World War II, lying in the snow in France with bullets flying, a bad round of golf was just a tiny speed bump in a man's life.

I looked again at Ryan, and then at my other sons, Jeff and Jon, who were lining up with Ryan to shout down the heckler, and I could sense the same connection that I shared with *my* dad.

And just like that, I relaxed and felt my timing come back. I surrendered to the moment and let my years of training play out the round. I no longer felt an attachment to the results.

I birdied six of the last 11 holes at Crooked Stick in that U.S. Senior Open, with my gallery loudly cheering every birdie putt. I birdied 17 and 18, my last two holes, and when my six-foot birdie putt fell on 18, you would have thought that I'd won the tournament!

That moment was my greatest moment in 60 years of playing the game, 48 of those professionally. There were thousands around that 18th green, waiting to see the stars, the big names. But the only ones I saw when I picked my ball up out of that cup were my friends and family, cheering and hollering along with the massive crowd. But my gallery's cheers were considerably louder than the others!

Sure, I'd missed the 36-hole cut by a mile, but I showed, on those last 11 holes, that I belonged.

So there you have it, the perfect example of how this game can take away, and then give back, sometimes in the span of one hole.

If there is one lesson learned from that experience, it's that there's a lot of power involved in our human connections, power that can transform our thinking and change our lives for the better.

I discovered that how I played golf really was not who I was after all—that my score did not define me. For that lesson, I'm thankful to the two who taught it to me that day at Crooked Stick—my son Ryan and my late dad, John Miller. Also among my "teachers" that day were Connie; my other sons, Jeffrey and Jonathan; and all of my friends who cheered as that birdie dropped on 18.

For the record, though, those first 25 holes still sting.

My career in golf has been filled with interesting and sometimes amazing experiences. It has provided synchronicities beyond belief and endless epiphanies and revelations.

I have to share a few of the more incredible happenings along the way: Here's a story illustrating the very fine line between fame and obscurity, a line drawn by sheer luck, fate, or whatever name you want to give to the unpredictable ways of chance.

In about 1964, I played and practiced most days at the golf complex at City Park in New Orleans, on the courses that I grew up playing. City Park was where the elite of the *persona non grata* congregated every day. Mafia figures; racetrack trainers, jockeys, and owners; every sort of hustler you could imagine; and gamblers and bookmakers all graced the premises. Many carried guns.

I grew up playing for big money, sometimes backed by one of these characters, sometimes on my own with 10 dollars in my pocket. You did not want to lose without the ability to pay off.

When you gambled on yourself at City Park, "big money" was defined as "more than you have in your pocket."

On the first tee you were always reminded that you were playing "whip out," meaning that if you lost you were expected to "whip out" your money on the spot. There was no owing.

Fortunately, I was the best player around and could play my way out of any jam that I got into. Plus, some of the Mafia guys liked me and semi-protected me.

The east course was the course that most of the money games were played on, even though the west course was an equally stern test. Both courses could stretch to about 7,000 yards, which in those days was considered pretty long, and both courses played to a par of 72.

I played the course almost every day, so I knew it backward and forward and would routinely shoot from two to four under par.

There was a nice cafeteria where every morning there would be 20 to 30 people having coffee and breakfast and lining up the day's games and wagers. This went on for an hour or so and then, after all of the bickering about who was playing whom and how many strokes were being given, the cafeteria emptied out and the group headed out to the first tee.

Well, one morning when all of the finagling was going on, a young twentysomething blond guy walked in the door. Nobody had ever seen him before. He came in and said, "I understand that there are some money games here. I'd like to get in on some of the action. Who is the best player here?"

A couple of the guys pointed to me. This kid, whose name was Don Parsons, said, "I'll play him nine holes for however much you can gather up, and I'm only going to use a 1 iron."

You may have heard Lee Trevino's funny line about the difficulty of hitting a 1 iron: as he held it up to the sky during a lightning storm, he told his playing partners, "Don't worry, it's safe. Even God can't hit a 1 iron!"

Needless to say, money came flying out of pockets, and when it got to $5,000 this kid said, "That'll do."

So off we went to the first tee of the east course, where I would be pretty certain to shoot 33 to 36 easily. And this guy, whom no one had ever seen, was going to play with only a 1 iron, on a golf course that he'd apparently never set foot on.

My attention was caught right away when his drive with his 1 iron ended up about 10 yards past my drive, which I hit pretty much as well as I could.

Then he got my full attention when he opened up the face of his 1 iron, making it look more like a 9 iron, and played this soft little drop-fade from 100 yards out to 15 feet from the hole.

Still, I figured there was no way that this guy could possibly have the diverse array of shots he would need to beat me for nine holes.

I was wrong. He shot 34 with his 1 iron. If I hadn't witnessed it, I would never have believed it. He could hit any shot with that club, even bunker shots, and putting was no problem whatsoever due to the fact that the loft on a one iron is not drastically different from the loft of a putter.

It was amazing, and my even par 36 lost by two strokes. I believe that the reason that I shot only even par was because

I was fascinated watching this guy shoot two under with a 1 iron on a pretty tough course that he was not familiar with.

Don Parsons stuck around for a few months after that and we became friends. He was the prototypical California beach boy—blond, good-looking, and built like an athlete. He was about 5'11", 170 pounds, and could drive it close to 300 yards—and in those days we played with persimmon wood drivers and much softer golf balls than what we play with today.

The guy was an incredible talent and he was smart, and no doubt would have had an extremely successful career on the PGA Tour.

But Lady Luck said no. He was planning to go to Q-School and qualify for the Tour when he hurt his back. I don't remember the circumstances, but it basically ended his quest because he just couldn't swing the same way that he did before the injury.

The last I heard he was a club pro somewhere in Connecticut.

There have been many stories like his—world-beaters who, for one reason or another, faded into golfing obscurity.

As I said, it takes a lot more that talent to make it in professional golf.

Sometimes golf can provide seemingly mystical experiences and stunning synchronicities. The real world of golf can sometimes mirror the story of Michael Murphy's best-selling classic, *Golf in the Kingdom*.

Synchronicity Stories

Here are a couple of examples of the extraordinary things that I have been a part of:

In about 1997, my oldest son Ryan had been thinking about getting a dog. One morning I was on my way to practice at Beau Chene Country Club, getting ready to head to qualifying school for the Champions Tour when my cell phone rang. It was Ryan. "Hey Dad, guess what?" he asked.

I just sort of unthinkingly blurted out (intuitively, in retrospect), "You got a dog!"

He said, "Yep, a little miniature Doberman puppy." So I half-jokingly asked, "What are you going to name him? Brutus?"

Ryan said, "No, better than that. I'm gonna name him Boom-Boom!"

So we talked for a few minutes and I went on to the club and started practicing. After a while, I worked my way up to hitting drivers.

Now, Beau Chene provided free tees to the members, and there was a big basket of them on the counter in the golf shop. They were all plain white tees, with no logo or anything on them. When a club gives the members free tees, the practice tees are full of them because the members just leave them on the ground. They were literally all over the place. (Curiously, when people have to buy them you can't find one anywhere!)

So I was hitting drivers, one after the other, and there were plain white tees everywhere all over the ground. At some point, I bent down to pick one up and started to tee it up when I noticed black writing on it.

I looked more closely and saw that it was personalized with two words on it. The two words were *Boom-Boom*.

I was pretty stunned, and started picking up tees all around the driving range and inspecting them. It soon became apparent that only one had this writing on it.

That experience was one of the more surprising and unlikely synchronicities that I've ever been a part of, and I have no idea what it meant.

As the noted synchronicity researcher and author David Peat says, it was "just a tear in the fabric of reality."

As a sidenote, Ryan ended up naming his puppy Jimi, and they enjoyed many years of friendship together.

Another somewhat "mystical" experience involved the elusive golfing "pot of gold"—the hole in one.

In the early 2000s, Connie and I were playing in a couples event at New Orleans Country Club with Mark and Mary Vitter, two of our close friends. Mark is a radiologist, a fine player, and a graduate of Notre Dame, and has a son who played on the Notre Dame golf team.

We were standing on the tee on the fifth hole and had to wait a bit for the group ahead to clear. In passing, I asked Mark how many holes in one he'd made. He said that in 47 years of playing the game he'd never had one. I could tell by his tone and demeanor that he really felt shortchanged by Lady Luck with regard to this golfing Holy Grail.

Because I could sense his genuine regret over never having made one, and knowing well his love of the game, I actually felt compassion for him.

Holes in one, after all, are largely a matter of luck. It takes a good shot to get close, but for the ball to actually go into the hole from so far away takes a little bit of good fortune.

We played the par-4 fifth hole and the par-4 sixth, forgetting entirely about the hole in one conversation. We got to the tee of the par-3 seventh hole at NOCC, and it was playing about 160 yards. Mark hit first, a 6 iron, and it never left the flag. A perfect shot. We didn't know how perfect until it landed about 10 feet short of the hole and rolled straight into the center of the cup as if guided by some remote-controlled device. And maybe it was.

Mark turned toward me—and I know he won't be embarrassed when he reads this—and there was a hint of tears in his eyes—tears of joy! I went over and congratulated him and hugged him. I was really happy for him, knowing what it meant.

Could that conversation on the fifth tee have been some kind of stimulant? Could my sincere compassion have opened some door? There's no way of knowing, but I'm suspicious.

That was the second time that something like that happened at NOCC with regard to a hole in one. About eight years before Mark's hole in one, Connie and I were playing with a dentist from out of town whom I was helping out with his golf swing.

When we arrived at the 14th tee, a long par-3, I asked the guy if he'd ever had an ace. He said no. He then proceeded to hit a 3 iron into the hole.

These kinds of events make you wonder, but after having been close friends with *Celestine Prophecy* author James Redfield for so many years, nothing surprises me anymore.

There very definitely seems to be, as David Peat says, an underlying fabric to our everyday reality that connects all things.

These unseen connections seem to pop to the surface every now and then, stimulated by heaven knows what. But as James says, the more you look for them the more you notice them, and the more often they appear.

Everything is connected; we just have to be opened to the view.

Golf has always been regarded as a gentleman's game, with strict adherence to the rules and etiquette. It is a game of honor and sportsmanship. There have been several instances where top professionals have called penalties on themselves, penalties that only they could have been aware of, that cost them tournament victories and lots of prize money.

To illustrate this code of honor among the game's top amateurs and professionals, I want to share a story from 1973.

I was in a Monday qualifier for the Western Open in Chicago, paired with two other pros and set to tee off early, something like 7:40 AM.

After warming up and arriving at the first tee, we were informed that our group would only be a twosome, as our third player had withdrawn with a bad back or something.

The starter told us to play away, and stepped back to the starters' tent. I was to tee off first.

As I teed the ball up and prepared to start my routine, I noticed the other player standing very close to me, which is highly unusual.

I kind of looked up and this player sort of whispered to me, "You know, we can both qualify today if you know what I mean."

I didn't look up. I just said, "Yep, if we play well enough."

I went ahead and hit my tee shot and not another word was said by this guy about what had been said on the first tee.

I tell this story because it stands out in my memory. I turned pro in 1967, so I have played professionally for 50 years, in countless tournaments and qualifiers.

That incident was the *only* time in all those years that I personally witnessed another golf professional openly attempting to cheat. I'm sure that there have been others, but it's the only one that I've ever witnessed. That's pretty remarkable, and a testament to how golf is so different.

I hope that with the changing times and moral values that the game retains its sacred code of honor, because it's one of the things that sets it apart and makes it an incredible teaching tool for young kids.

In one of my earlier books I posed this question: "Have you ever known of a 15-year-old avid golfer who gets in trouble?" I haven't.

Debunking some harmful clichés and myths

There are several clichés and myths about the golf swing that do great harm to the average golfer. You would think that by now these well-meaning but harmful "tips" would stop appearing in golfing publications, but they continue to be published in magazines and taught by many golf instructors, most of whom have little or no formal or proper training.

1. **Keep your head still.** This one is the classic. After being told this, you'll see the beginner try to swing while attempting to keep his head totally still, locked and frozen to the point that there is hardly any degree of shoulder turn. There's no freedom in the swing. We call this being "ball bound." While it is true that the head acts as the "hub" of the swing as the torso, shoulders, and hips rotate around it, there is a proper way to express this concept. Trying too hard to keep the head completely still causes rigidity and tension and prevents a free rotation. It limits mobility. A much better way to say this is, "Don't let your head move too much when you swing." That way, you still have freedom to rotate around the hub. Watch most world class players as they swing and you'll see some head movement, albeit minimal, as they rotate with a definite sense and feeling

of freedom. Great players exhibit no rigidity or tension when they swing.

2. **Keep your left arm straight.** Another timeless one. This advice results in the golfer stiffening his left arm to the point that it is so tense and rigid that there is no chance of hinging the wrist during the backswing. It also inhibits the shoulder turn by once again destroying any freedom to move with fluidity. There is a big difference between stiff and straight. The better way to convey this is to say "keep the left arm extended but not stiff." This way the width of swing is preserved without tension.

3. **Stay down through impact.** This tip is very harmful. It gives the player the impression that he must keep his head in place and his eyes glued to the ball well into his follow through. This results in a "blocking out" of the body rotation on the downswing and the subsequent deceleration of the golf club. It causes the hands to release prematurely on the downswing and a casting of the club. Depending on where the player's weight is on the downswing, the resultant shot could be "thin" or "fat." Much better to say, "Stay in your posture through impact." Maintaining posture increases chances for solid contact with the ball, and allows the club to continue to accelerate.

4. **Swaying.** You hear this one all the time. Instead of rotating, the player moves laterally back and forth, sliding instead of turning. But there is a universal misconception about swaying. Bolt told me that Hogan said that you're only swaying if the inside of your right foot leaves the ground. Tommy would say to me repeatedly, "Son, keep your spikes in the ground, that's what they're for!" If all of your spikes stay in the ground (or your right foot stays solidly planted), you can shift your weight as much as you'd like.

   A great example is two-time U.S. Open champ Curtis Strange, who had a pronounced lateral move on his backswing as he shifted his weight. But his right foot was rock solid in its connection to the ground.

   If you're too intent on not swaying, you run the risk of failing to adequately shift weight to the right side, which may result in a reverse weight shift and the resultant loss of power and an increased chance of non-solid contact.

5. **"My timing is off!"** Just about anyone who has ever played the game has uttered (or muttered) this golfing cliché. But how many golfers even know what they mean by it? Let me clear it up.

   Timing is the timing, or synchronization, of the movements of the golf club and your body. Ken Venturi once said that when a golfer hits a poor shot, either the club outraces the body or the body outraces the club.

In an efficient golf swing, the movements must be synchronized. And by achieving the positions that make up the geometry that Hogan figured out, that synchronization is guaranteed.

If the positions are missed, then the body must either speed up or slow down in order to get back on track, or the delivery of the club to the ball will have to be accelerated or slowed down.

When the positions are spot on, timing doesn't even enter the equation. (And that's what Ben Hogan was after, a swing that did not rely on timing.)

The Value of the Short Game—100 Yards In

Hogan did not like putting. He said that he wanted to be remembered as a great ball striker, not a great putter. He once said this to Freddie Haas, who had offered to help Hogan with his putting. He even said that golf should abolish putting—that points should be awarded on the basis of how many greens in regulation the golfer hit and proximity to the hole.

But when Hogan was winning all those tournaments he was a very good putter, especially from six feet and under.

It was only late in his career that he experienced severe putting problems, which, by his own account, were the result of nerves that he was not able to control, largely due to residual effects from the horrific car wreck he was involved in on February 2, 1949. He also had deteriorating vision in his left eye, also due to damage sustained in that wreck.

Hogan hit such a high percentage of greens in regulation that he didn't have to chip or pitch all that much, but Freddie Haas told me that Hogan had a very good touch around the greens.

They didn't keep detailed stats in those days, but if they had I'd love to see Hogan's percentage of greens hit in regulation. It would have easily eclipsed the percentage of today's best players.

Aside from improving your full swing technique, there are two ways that you can significantly lower your scoring and your handicap: by getting serious about learning better course management, and by working hard on your short game.

From 100 yards in, you need to practice all kinds of shots from all kinds of different lies from a wide variety of distances. A sharp short game is worth its weight in gold and is largely ignored by the average golfer, who would rather stand on the range and whale away at the driver.

I personally made the mistake of not putting enough time into short-game practice when I was playing competitively. As I prepared to start my playing career, I thought that I had a great short game, and I did…around my familiar hometown courses. Consequently, I spent most of my practice time beating balls on the range. So when I started playing professionally at golf courses around the different parts of the country, with different grasses and different terrains, I found that my short game, in reality, was not actually all that good compared with world-class players.

These guys had great short games everywhere, no matter the type of grass or terrain they were playing.

I would routinely go around hitting 13 to 15 greens in regulation and shooting 72 and 73 while the top players would hit 11 greens and shoot 68 or 69. And when they would hit 15 greens they'd often come in shooting 65 or 66.

I can tell you that if I had it to do over again I would spend 80 percent of my practice time on all varieties of shots from 100 yards in. And I preach this to every young aspiring golfer that I advise.

Reading Your Lie

This is a very important factor when deciding what type of shot to play and which club to use. Reading the lie of the ball might be the most overlooked and underestimated part of shot planning, not only from 100 yards in but for all golf shots.

Of course, many casual players improve their lies and therefore always have a good one with the ball sitting up. But I would recommend that all players learn to play the ball as it lies. It will make you a better player in the long run.

The first thing to look for is if there is any grass that will be between the ball and the clubface when you address the ball. Take note of the thickness of the grass and the length of the blades and in which direction the blades are lying. The blades of grass might be toward the clubface or away from it or to one side or the other. These factors make a difference and will help to determine how the flight of the ball will be affected.

If the ball is sitting up nicely on the grass with no grass between the ball and club, you can expect the flight of the ball not to be affected at all. But if there is grass there, usually when your ball is lying in the rough off of the fairway, then you need to allow for how the flight might be affected.

When there is grass between the ball and the clubface, most of the time you're going to get some degree of a "flier." A flier is when the clubface can't contact the ball cleanly and considerably less backspin is imparted to the ball. The ball takes off faster and flies farther than normal—hence the term *flier*. A flier will roll out much farther.

You have to be careful when assessing the lie of the ball and if the circumstances for a probable flier are there, you'll want to take at least one less club for the shot than you normally would. And if you're downwind, the result will be exaggerated.

Now, if there is a *lot* of thick grass between the ball and clubface, the ball is not going to travel as far as usual with the particular club you're going to use. The club won't get to the ball to compress it and the grass will slow down the clubhead speed.

Two other considerations when assessing these lies in high grass: if the blades of grass are growing/lying against the clubface, the flier effect typically won't be as great, and conversely if the grass is growing/lying toward the ball you'll typically get the full effect of the flier.

If you find your ball in a divot in the fairway, the best way to maximize your chances is to take one more club, choke it down an inch or two, and play the ball back in your stance. You want to make sure that you contact the ball first, preferably just below the equator of the ball.

The same applies to a lie that is sitting down in the fairway, instead of sitting up nicely. It's hard to get the sweet spot on the back of the ball when it's sitting down in a sort of depression. Playing the ball back in your stance a bit and choking down a half inch will result in a cleaner, crisper strike and minimize the chances of hitting behind the ball.

2016 Masters

I'm sitting here at the breakfast table of our rental house in Kiawah Island, South Carolina, where Connie and I come every year for a little R&R with James and Salle Redfield.

James and I are working, as we do early every morning, before the day's activities of golf, eating, and shopping begin.

I am working on this book and James (his fans will be excited to learn) is working on a sequel to *The Celestine Prophecy*.

It's the morning after the 2016 Masters, the morning after Jordan Spieth's epic meltdown.

Lying in bed early this morning, it hit me that what the world witnessed during Spieth's disastrous back nine was a total confirmation and validation of what Ben Hogan discovered and what this book is all about.

Spieth lost control of his golf swing. Under the pressure cooker that is the final nine of a major championship, his in-swing adjustments kept missing the mark.

Spieth's meltdown was a classic example of a golf swing that sometimes requires in-swing adjustments, however slight. It's a great, effective golf swing that produces high-quality golf shots most of the time, but the fact is that his putting makes up for his less-than-stellar ball striking.

I'm not saying that he's a bad ball striker. He hits great golf shots. But take a look at his GIR (greens in regulation) stats.

Incredibly, at the time of this writing, Jordan Spieth is 165th on the PGA Tour in greens in regulation. And this is the No. 1 or No. 2 ranked player in the world!

In the final round of the Masters, Spieth's golf swing got off track, and under the severest of pressures he couldn't find the compensations needed to control the accuracy of his shots.

If Jordan can make a few small tweaks to improve the geometry of his swing, the game's best putter will be a solid favorite to shatter Jack Nicklaus' record of 18 major championship victories.

Spieth has it all, he just needs a small tweak in his mechanics so that he never has to depend on and require in-swing adjustments.

With a 5-shot lead and 9 holes to play, do you think Ben Hogan would have shot 41 on that back 9, hitting 3 greens in regulation?

Hogan, unlike every other great player, never had a late tournament collapse. Why? Because pressure didn't bother his swing. It was totally efficient and did not rely on the timing of in-swing adjustments.

UNPUBLISHED HOGAN STORIES

MOST LIKELY YOU'VE heard many of the Hogan stories that have become part of the lore of golf's great history. Many of those stories are humorous because of the man's reputation as a cold-blooded killer on the golf course and because of his intense concentration and virtual exclusion of everything and everyone around him, save for the shot at hand.

Many of those stories have been somewhat embellished through the years for effect, but then again many are exactly true.

Everyone, especially Hogan fans, loves to read the Hogan stories because they offer some insight into the workings of this interesting man's mind.

Throughout this book are interspersed many of the more popular stories that have contributed to the Hogan legend, but I thought that I should include a section of unpublished stories and anecdotes that have never appeared in print and that only a handful of people have knowledge of.

On Hogan the Fierce Competitor

Tom Smith, a friend of mine in Highlands, North Carolina, is a longtime PGA golf professional who as a club pro was a member of the Hogan staff for many years starting in about 1980.

We got to know each other when we played a round together at Atlanta Athletic Club when Connie and Tom's wife, Kay, were playing the Women's Southern Amateur Championship at Capitol City Club in Atlanta.

Tom is a great guy, a heck of a good player, and has a treasure trove of golf stories from his many years in the business.

Every year, once a year, all of the Ben Hogan staff professionals would be invited to Fort Worth to tour the factory, view the new products, and mingle with the man himself. There was a huge dinner where Hogan would usually give a talk.

Sometimes Hogan would even play with some of the pros and hit balls with them at Shady Oaks, Hogan's hangout.

Tom told me a story about how late one afternoon during one of those yearly get-togethers he was sitting at a table drinking wine with Hogan, a couple of other club professionals and one or two Tour players, and Butch Harmon.

This was before Harmon became famous as a teacher, but his father, Claude Harmon, had been a close friend of Hogan's back in their tour days.

The conversation was light, everyone was in a good mood with an assist from the wine, and the talk centered around golf in general and the new Hogan products.

At some point in the conversation Butch Harmon said, "Mr. Hogan, I'm curious. Considering all of the courses you've played through all of these years, what is your all-time favorite hole? Which hole did you like the most"?

Suddenly the table went silent and Hogan's demeanor transformed. It was if the air had been sucked out of the room. Hogan could do that to his surroundings. Those hawklike, blue-gray eyes could bore right through to your soul, and many strong personalities would wilt under the intense stare that he could manifest.

A tense minute went by without a word as the entire table waited for a response. Quite often Hogan would not answer a question right away. He would carefully consider the question and the ramifications of his answer before he would respond.

After what seemed like an eternity, Hogan focused his stare on Harmon, and according to Tom, here is exactly what he said:

"Butch, let me tell you something. I *hated* every golf hole that I've ever played. To me, a golf hole is the enemy, and I want to defeat it. You ask me which holes I've liked? I hated them all."

Tom said that Hogan said those words with such force, such conviction, that no one said a word. The conversation quickly shifted gears, but needless to say all of those present were stunned at the obvious ferocity of Hogan's short diatribe.

That story shows the level of competitiveness that made Hogan perhaps the toughest competitor ever, in any sport. It was part and parcel of the whole package that enabled a man small in stature to become such a giant in his sport.

On Hogan's Grips

Tom also shared this story about the unique features of the golf grips that Hogan had on his clubs. He said that one day during one of those yearly visits to Fort Worth he was hitting balls with Hogan on Hogan's favorite practice area at Shady Oaks, on what's called the Little Nine.

At one point Hogan handed one of his clubs to Tom and explained how important it is to have the hands placed properly on the club.

The grip had to be neutral, a position that most people would call a "weak" grip. The emphasis of pressure on the club should be on the last three fingers of the left hand and on the middle two fingers of the right. The right index finger is placed on the club as if in a trigger position, but with almost no pressure. The right thumb[6] is putting no pressure on the club and is almost off of the club. Hogan, in fact, hit balls with his right thumb raised slightly above the grip, not

6. For more on the importance of the right thumb, refer to the Tom Moore story on page 204.

touching it at all. The hands should feel as if they are welded together and can function only as one singular unit.

Hogan used all-cord grips and they had a reminder built onto the bottom right of the grip at the 5 o'clock position. A reminder is a thin, thread-like ribbing that runs down the length of the bottom of the grip. Normally the reminder is at the bottom center, at what would be at the 6 o'clock position. When you order new clubs or have your present set re-gripped, you can specify having grips with reminders installed or not. The reminders ensured Hogan of having the same feel all of the time and also of having the hands in the exact same correct (for him) position every time.

All-cord grips are very rough on the hands and unless you practice a lot with them long-term, your hands can get pretty roughed up. Hogan's hands, as you can imagine, were very heavily callused.

Someone once asked Hogan if his hands ever hurt from all of the practicing that he did, and his response was, "Your hands only hurt when you're doing something you don't like to do." Such was his devotion to and love for practicing.

Finally, about Hogan's hands, let's dispel a long-believed myth that Ben Hogan was a lefty who played golf right-handed. Hogan was right-handed.

Hogan believed that the way you put your hands on the club was the most important fundamental of the game. It connects the golfer's body to the golf club, and if held incorrectly it sets up, right from the start, the need for all sorts of compensations.

Hogan once said, "Get a good grip and get good posture, and go practice."

Tom Smith told me that there was a club repair guru in Atlanta that he knew and would use for work on members' clubs when he was a club pro. He said that one day he was in the shop waiting for some clubs to be regripped when he spied a set of Hogan Apex irons leaning against the wall. Out of curiosity he picked up one of the irons and when he set it down and gripped it he felt the reminder. To his great surprise the reminder was in the 5 o'clock position, just like Hogan's!

Tom said that he asked Jerry who the clubs belonged to and Jerry said, "Why do you ask?" So Tom told him about the reminders and then Jerry said, "Oh, those were Larry Nelson's."

Larry Nelson won 10 times on the PGA Tour, including 3 majors, and 19 times on the Champions Tour.

At one time he played Hogan clubs. Obviously at some point either Hogan shared his reminder secret with Larry, or Larry got wind of it in some way.

Partly responsible for Nelson's tremendous record as a Tour player was the fact that he didn't have a two-way miss.

Not coincidentally, given his Hogan connections, Larry never hooked it. When you know that you can only miss a shot one way, the game is greatly simplified. Just ask Tiger.

In one of our conversations Tom Smith also talked about the sound of Hogan's golf shots, specifically the sound that was made when Hogan's club impacted the golf ball.

A TIP FOR CORRECT ALIGNMENT

This great tip is one that I evolved from Hogan's grip reminder, which he had placed in a specific location on the underside of all of his grips.

This enabled him to hold the club in precisely the same way every time, and it was placed in the position that was exactly appropriate for the stock drop-fade that he liked to play on most shots.

But for you, the reader, who aspires to hit the ball consistently straight on most shots, my tip will greatly encourage that ability.

When you get a new set of clubs, or when getting your present set regripped, have the grips installed so that the label or grip logo is exactly on top of the grip, so that you're looking straight down at that label or logo when placing the club behind the ball.

Make sure that the installer has the leading edge of your clubs exactly straight in relation to the label/logo of the grips.

This way, when you address the ball and you're looking straight down at the label/logo of your grip, you will be assured that your clubface is square to where you're aiming.

I and many other pros do this with our clubs. It takes the guesswork out of wondering if everything is aligned accurately.

Another benefit is that it gives you a consistent visual reference to make sure that your hands are placed properly on the club—in a neutral position with your palms perpendicular to your target line. And when your clubface is aligned properly, it makes it much easier to get the body lines (feet, knees, hips, and shoulders) straight.

This feature has been written about and referred to many times, but no one has ventured to say why Hogan's impact sound was so unusual.

I'd like to offer my thoughts on the subject and put forth a theory, a theory sprouted from a seed planted by Hogan himself.

Earlier we talked about Hogan reading somewhere in a physics book about the law of acceleration. He read and believed that if an object that struck another object traveled faster *after* impact than it did *at* impact, the object that was struck would go straighter and farther than if the object striking it did not achieve that greater speed after impact.

As with the principle of board-breaking in karate we discussed earlier, I believe that Hogan applied the same method to striking a golf ball. I believe that he was trying to swing through an imaginary ball that was lying a few inches in front of the real one, thereby ensuring, just like in karate, that his club was still accelerating as it contacted the real ball.

This idea would explain why his impact sound was so different, because his impact with the ball was more forceful than anyone else's.

Additionally, to add to the equation, Hogan made extraordinarily solid contact with the golf ball, a result of his extensive practice habits.

Many people have commented on how the sweet spot worn out on the face of his clubs was the size of a dime, as opposed to most other players whose sweet spot is larger, indicating a less precise point of contact.

All of this contributed to explaining how Hogan, given his smallish stature, could hit the ball so far with the equipment he used.

This imaginary ball technique reminds me of something I did with my sons when they were little and just getting into playing various sports. It was along the same lines of reaching for a higher goal, exceeding the ordinary.

I would draw a line on a wall and ask them to jump up and touch the line. I would increase the height until they maxed out on how high they could jump. Then I drew one a bit higher.

Then I would tell them to gather their strength, concentrate, and try with all their might to reach that line. They did it, proving that you can always get a little better with the right degree of intention and effort.

Hogan used that same extra-effort method to get his club to reach a greater speed.

Palmetto Golf Club

Palmetto Golf Club in Aiken, South Carolina, founded in 1892, is the second-oldest continuously operated 18 hole golf course in the United States, second only to Chicago Golf Club.

The course has been played by a veritable who's who not only from the world of golf, but from the worlds of entertainment, politics, and even royalty.

The Palmetto Pro-Am (officially the Devereux Milburn) was played from 1945 to 1953 the week before the Masters, and all of the top professionals (and amateurs) would play in the event as preparation for the first major championship of the year.

Through the years, the Palmetto Pro-Am was won by the likes of Byron Nelson, Sam Snead, Ben Hogan, and many other top players from that era.

The course was a great tune-up for the Masters, with its lightning-fast, undulating greens and fairways. Palmetto also features small, crowned greens, which afford professionals a great way to work on their iron-game accuracy.

Hogan called holes 3, 4, and 5 the three greatest consecutive par-4s in golf.

Tom Moore, recently retired, served as director of golf and general manager of Palmetto for over 30 years, and is one of only eight men to serve as Palmetto's head professional in its 125-year history.

Tom is now professional emeritus at the club and teaches almost daily. He is considered the dean of golf professionals in the Aiken/Augusta area.

He is considered one of the game's premier instructors and has brought along a host of fine players, including current PGA Tour players Kevin Kisner and Scott Brown.

Tom Moore is also mostly responsible for creating the History Room at Palmetto, which features memorabilia and artifacts dating back to the early 1900s.

Pictures, golf clubs, golf balls, signed papers, telegrams—you name it, it's in there. There are even gutta percha golf balls that through the years have turned up on the course, balls that were played in the early part of the last century.

Anyone interested in the history of the game should visit the History Room at Palmetto.

I've visited with Tom a few times, twice during the writing of this book, to learn more about the history of Palmetto and particularly about Ben Hogan.

Tom is a reserved man who, like Hogan, thinks before he speaks. He weighs your questions carefully and then answers with direct, even tones. The man is a treasure trove of golfing lore and information, but you have to prod him carefully for it.

Hogan was a yearly participant at Palmetto in the tournament that served as the final tune-up for the Masters, because he considered the course to be perfect for preparing for the fast and undulating greens of Augusta National.

Even the fairways simulated those of the Masters course. The biggest difference was the size of the greens, with Palmetto featuring small greens compared with Augusta's massive ones.

However, that made Palmetto even more effective as a training ground because Palmetto demanded precise iron play, which is vital at the Masters. If your iron game is off at the Masters you have no chance, because you're going to leave yourself in positions that almost guarantee a host of three putts on the massive and wildly undulating greens.

Tom had some stories about Hogan during the years that he competed at Palmetto, and I was all ears as he slowly pulled them from his memory bank.

Tom told a story that illustrated the meticulous way that Hogan prepared for competition.

On the morning before one of the Palmetto pro-ams, Jack Parker, a friend of Hogan's and one of Palmetto's higher-ups, was at the club and asking if Hogan was around. It was early and it was extremely foggy. Someone told him that Hogan was out on the course practicing alone, as was his custom. Parker was told that Hogan was probably out somewhere around the 13th hole.

Parker got in his car and drove out to that area looking for Hogan and caught a glimpse through the fog of someone hitting approach shots to the 13th green.

He got out of his car and walked toward the green and through the heavy fog he could hear thump after thump as balls landed on the green. As he got closer he could see the balls, but they were clustered in two distinct areas, one in the far back right portion of the green and the other in the far back left.

When Hogan finally walked up to the green he was greeted by Parker and after exchanging pleasantries Parker asked him why all the balls were clustered around the back left and right portions of the green when the pin was in the front middle of it.

Hogan's reply was that every year that's where the pin locations were in the actual tournament. That story shows the depth of Hogan's practice and preparation.

He was avant garde when it came to practice; he practically invented it.

The Palmetto Pro-Am featured most of the top professionals of the era and also a number of world class amateurs.

Two of the more well-known amateurs and members of Palmetto were Bobby Knowles and Bobby Goodyear (of *the* Goodyear family). The two were friends of and frequent playing partners of Hogan's.

Bobby Knowles was an accomplished amateur who was ranked fifth in the world at one point. Among his victories were the Massachusetts Amateur, the New England Amateur, and the French Amateur. He was selected to and played on a winning Walker Cup team and played in two Masters tournaments as an amateur.

Tom Moore tells the following story about Hogan.

One year Hogan played a practice round with his pals Goodyear and Knowles and another unnamed local amateur.

After the round the men were having lunch in the grill and at some point one of them asked Hogan if he could offer some observations about their respective swings and golf games in general.

Here's how Hogan responded, and his opening response ended that conversation abruptly. He said, "Bobby, if I hit the ball like you I think I'd find another sport to play." This to the fifth-ranked amateur in the country!

Now, Hogan may have very well been sticking the needle to Knowles, but you can bet that there was more than a measure of seriousness involved. Hogan was on such a higher level of ball striking than all other professionals, let alone an amateur (albeit one of the top ones), that what he considered inferior ball striking was a very relative observation.

And, of course, the secret of scoring in golf lies in relativity. For example, if a PGA Tour player hits a bad 7 iron shot, the ball may end up 25 to 30 feet from the hole.

If a 10-handicap amateur hits a bad 7 iron it may end up 50 feet from the hole. If a 20-handicapper hits the same club poorly it likely will end up in a greenside bunker or worse. And on and on.

The point is, the secret to scoring in golf is how *good* your bad shots are. Even the 20-handicapper can occasionally hit a shot every bit as good as a tour player, but the difference is the frequency with which that happens, and where the poor shots finish.

The tour player hits really good shots with great frequency and his misses are usually not all that bad.

I've played in hundreds of pro-ams with every sort of golfer imaginable, and I've seen fantastic shots by very bad golfers.

I've also seen some of the world's top-ranked golfers hit shots that would embarrass a 20-handicapper. It's all about the frequency and quality.

In all of those hundreds of pro-ams I've played in, I have to share what might be my funniest pro-am moment.

It was in the Houston Open Pro-Am, 1976, at The Woodlands. My D player, which means the highest handicapper on the team, supposedly had a 22 handicap, but was obviously much higher. He was a very nice, social guy, but he rarely got the ball off the ground and never really contributed to the team effort or even finished a hole.

As we walked off of the final green exchanging pleasantries, this guy came over to me, puts his arm on my shoulder, and said, "You know, I can play a lot better than that, but I never seem to." He was dead serious.

I had to think about it for a minute and then had to stifle my laughter, because I realized that he was serious.

When you think about it, two things can be gleaned from that—two things that make up the psychological fabric of the game.

First, it illustrates that most high handicappers, however badly they play, *want* to play well really badly. Second, almost every golfer is somewhat delusional.

James Redfield says that his father used to tell him, "James, your problem is that you think you're much better than you are!"

One interesting thing about Ben Hogan was that he played without ego. He conducted his life with humility and was above all a gentleman, putting great emphasis on good manners, personal appearance, and hygiene. Hogan considered the rules to be sacred, and wouldn't hesitate to point out transgressions. He even called out his protégé and close friend Tommy Bolt once. They were practicing the day before a tournament and at some point Hogan looked at one of Tommy's irons. He ran his fingers down the club face and almost cut his fingers on the grooves of the iron. The grooves had been "dug out" a bit, making them deeper and thus able to impart more spin to the ball, which of course is not legal. In those days many players did this, rationalizing that over time the grooves wear down and need to be refurbished. But they tended to overdo it.

Hogan told Tommy that he needed to change irons before the tournament started or else he, Hogan, was not going to play. Bolt complied. Such was Hogan's respect for the rules.

When he teed it up he became an assassin, a fierce competitor, but even so he was always gracious in defeat and congratulatory to his victorious opponents.

He was always respectful in the presence of women and did not tolerate others who lacked that respectful behavior.

Hogan *never* bragged about his accomplishments, great as they were.

The best way to describe Ben Hogan is that he was a gentleman warrior.

Tom Moore told this story about when the MacGregor Company signed Hogan up to play their equipment. This was early in Hogan's career before the Ben Hogan company existed.

The new MacGregor clubs featured extremely small club heads, much smaller than those of the other leading manufacturers of that time.

So the president of MacGregor proudly presented Hogan with his new clubs, telling him that he was proud to have him on staff and that he was expected to play the new models. Having Hogan playing their clubs would be a huge boost for sales.

When Hogan took a look at those clubs with their ultra-small heads, he told the MacGregor president that there was no way that he could play with them.

The president told Hogan that he had to play them because it would generate tremendous sales.

Hogan said, "You're gonna have to find someone better than me to hit these clubs, because I can't find the sweet spot."

And that was the beginning of the Ben Hogan Golf Company!

There was another story from early in Hogan's career, when the Hershey Open was played at Hershey Country Club in Hershey, Pennsylvania. At the time it was a major Tour stop.

Hogan was not well known at the time, especially in that part of the country. At the time of this particular Hershey Open, Henry Picard, who was instrumental in curing Hogan's chronic hook and turning his game around, was the head professional at Hershey Country Club.

Right before the start of the tournament one of the star players of the day, Ralph Guldahl, had to pull out of the tournament.

Henry Picard plugged the little-known Hogan into the field as Guldahl's replacement, much to the consternation of the members at Hershey and the tournament committee. They were not happy with having an unknown thrust into their illustrious field.

Well, all Hogan did was shoot a course-record 62 in one round on his way to winning the tournament by 12 strokes, lapping the field.

Ben Hogan always credited Henry Picard with putting his game on track and considered Picard to be a close friend and mentor.

The Right Thumb

When I sat down to interview Tom Moore, I told him that I was doing a book about everything that Tommy Bolt had taught me that Hogan had taught him. I didn't say anything about a secret.

During the course of the interview we talked about the importance that Hogan placed on the correct positioning and usage of the hands in the golf swing.

I told Tom about the drill that Hogan did where he would hit ball after ball in succession with a 5 iron, going straight from the finish of the swing back to the address position and repeating this a number of times, *without allowing his hands to change position on the club at all.*

It is extremely difficult to do and performing this drill on a consistent basis greatly increases the control one has over the club.

Tom didn't know that Hogan had done this but told me about another drill that Hogan used as a practice tool, and even did it occasionally when hitting shots in competition.

Tom feels so strongly about the merits of this drill that he believes that it was Hogan's secret.

I didn't tell him that it was just another feature of the effectiveness of Hogan's swing.

Nonetheless, I believe that the drill can enhance anyone's golf swing and I strongly suggest that you try it.

Hogan would practice hitting shots with his right thumb completely off of the club, hovering it about an inch directly above the grip of the club. Also, the right index finger is touching the grip, but ever so slightly with no pressure applied to the grip.

This accomplishes two important things.

First, it forces the emphasis of grip pressure to be in the right places, namely the last three, and particularly the middle two fingers of the right hand.

Second, and I believe more important, it prevents any possibility of the right thumb applying downward pressure on the shaft at the beginning of the downswing. Applying downward pressure at this stage of the swing encourages "casting" of the clubhead, which erases the energy stored in the angle between the shaft of the club and the left arm.

In other words, there is very little lag on the downswing and a serious loss of clubhead speed and hence power.

Having the right thumb off of the grip also lessens the chance of its inhibiting the hinging of the right wrist on the backswing.

This drill certainly contributed to Hogan's ability to generate extraordinary power for a man of his rather diminutive size.

You can get a sense of this Hogan fundamental by checking out pages 27 and 31 in Hogan's *Five Lessons*.

Tom Moore went on to say that if you want to add significant power to your swing, you should perform this drill religiously.

I use this drill myself and find it particularly effective when playing pitch shots from 10 to 50 yards. On these shots it frees up the hinging of the wrists by reducing pressure on the shaft. Most of the time when a player chunks or thins these shots it's a result of tension in the hands/wrists. Short-game shots rely a great deal on feel and touch, and tension brought on by excessive grip pressure—or pressure in the wrong place—destroys that feel.

The 1967 Ryder Cup Matches, Champions Golf Club, Houston, Texas

This is a great, little-known story involving two giants of the game that occurred at the 1967 Ryder Cup matches.

Europe was still using the small British golf ball, 1.62 inches in diameter, as opposed to the American ball, which measured (and still does) 1.68 inches. The British ball, as it was referred to, would travel a good 15–20 yards farther.

In later years, the ball would become standardized to the 1.68-inch diameter and the small ball eventually disappeared and became extinct.

But at that 1967 Ryder Cup the choice of ball was optional.

Ben Hogan was the captain that year, and the tough little Texan was serving as not only captain and coach, but disciplinarian as well, insisting on strict curfews and such.

Because of the considerable distance advantage that the Europeans would have, Hogan, before the start of the first practice round, ordered his charges to use the smaller ball so that they would get used to it.

Arnold Palmer, one of Hogan's top players, lightheartedly voiced dissatisfaction with this decision, telling Hogan that he'd brought none of the smaller balls with him.

Hogan's reply: "Who said you're playing?" And he wasn't kidding.

Of course, Palmer complied and indeed played as the Americans trounced the Europeans in one of the more lopsided Ryder Cups in the long history of the matches.

To be fair, the Europeans have more than evened the score as the number of great European players has dramatically increased over the last 30 years.

It was at that same Ryder Cup in 1967 that Hogan stood up at the opening ceremony and famously introduced his team this way: "Ladies and gentlemen, I introduce to you the finest players in the world."

It was a stunningly pointed move on Hogan's part and underscored his ultracompetitive nature. Hogan took no prisoners.

ENCOUNTERS WITH THE GREATS: MEMORIES AND STORIES FROM 50 YEARS AS A GOLF PROFESSIONAL

WHEN I RELUCTANTLY and unfortunately had to interrupt my playing career on the PGA Tour, I left with—as the old saying goes—"an empty money clip and a pocketful of memories."

I say unfortunately because I was just beginning to "get it," meaning that I was beginning to learn how to play under the pressure of competitive golf at the highest level.

It's a process, sometimes a long one, and you have to have the will and desire to persevere, you have to have the talent, and you have to have the circumstances that allow you to persevere.

As far as the pocketful of memories, you can't put a price on that value. The friendships, the connections, the stories…they offer a lifetime of comfort, joy, regret, and personal feelings of accomplishment, just for having been there.

When I turned pro and went to work for Jim Hart at Lakewood Country Club in New Orleans, it was at a time when the PGA Tour played the New Orleans Open there.

So I had a ringside seat to observe some of history's greatest players in their prime. Palmer, Nicklaus, Player, Trevino, and others.

I'll recount some of those observations and encounters a little later, but I want to begin by fast-forwarding a few years to the time when I played my very first tournament as a member of the PGA Tour.

It was called the Citrus Invitational, at Rio Pinar Country Club in Orlando, Florida, and it was the forerunner of Arnold Palmer's Bay Hill Invitational.

It was my first Tour event, and I have to admit that I was not only nervous, but I was in awe. Here I was competing against the very same players that a few years earlier I was running errands for as the assistant pro at Lakewood.

Arnold Palmer himself was in the field, and he had just been voted Athlete of the Year by the Associated Press.

I had one of those early tee times that we unknowns were saddled with, something like 7:30 AM. Palmer, like the other top players, had a later, more reasonable 12-something time.

But Palmer, who was expected that evening in New York City at the AP awards ceremony, asked the tournament committee to send him out early so that he could hop in his jet and get to New York for the awards dinner. The committee, of course, complied.

So Palmer got the early tee time, and as luck would have it, he was in a pairing with two nobodys *right behind* my group of nobodys.

Needless to say, it was an incredible and unnerving experience. Every green that we approached had more than 5,000 people surrounding it as they waited for the King.

It was a raucous, noisy spectacle, and furthermore, the guys in my group, including me, were more concerned with looking back to see what Arnie was doing than with what we were doing.

I remember shooting 74 that day, which was respectable under the circumstances but not exactly a score that would fare well against the world-class field.

But, there was a moment in the round that I'll never forget. It was a mind-blowing, profound experience. It was on the 15th hole, a par-5.

I had about an 80-yard wedge shot to the green for my third shot, and as was the case all the way around the course the throngs were around the green waiting for their hero.

I hit my wedge shot perfectly, and it carried a few feet past the hole and spun back to about two feet, just missing the hole. The crowd started screaming, whooping, and hollering, and I swear the hair on my arms stood up. It was unlike anything that I'd ever experienced. It was an adrenaline rush. I tapped in for birdie as the crowd quieted and refocused on why they were there, to see Arnie.

It was not until that evening at dinner with one of my rookie traveling mates that it hit me.

Arnold Palmer experiences that all day, every day, on every good shot that he hits, and he hits a lot of good shots!

I can see why that kind of adrenaline rush could get to be addictive, and how it can spur a player on to great performances, but when it happens for the first time it leaves you briefly shaken. Ten thousand people screaming and applauding your good shot can get you pumped for sure!

The other thing that struck me about that experience was the fact that having almost 10,000 people surrounding every green, standing 20 people deep, makes it almost impossible to miss the green with your approach shot. You can bet that Palmer, Nicklaus, and Tiger Woods had their greens in regulation stats boosted more than a little by having those huge galleries.

During my time working at Lakewood and getting to watch the world's best players up close, there were many memorable experiences.

When Jack Nicklaus would arrive at Lakewood for the tournament, his first stop was the golf shop. He would come in and greet Jim Hart and myself, and would then pull out a pen and notepad and ask Jim for the names of the caddiemaster, the club manager, the receptionist, and the locker room attendants and dining room waiters and waitresses. He wanted to be able to address them by their names when he was in and around the club. A personal touch.

Pretty impressive.

Now this is not a knock on Jack, because it was a classy thing to do, and everyone's mind does not work the same. But when Arnold Palmer got to the club, he *remembered* everyone's name from previous years.

I've heard other stories about Palmer's legendary memory. He just had a knack for remembering names. The point of the story is that those two giants of the game, while going about things in different ways, showed lots of class by making the effort to make the everyday employees at Lakewood feel special.

There was always a kind of spiritual, almost mystical aspect to Arnold Palmer's tournament play.

He had a flair for the dramatic, with comeback wins the norm. Late charges with birdie streaks seemed to happen frequently, and there were even media accounts of Palmer "willing" the ball into the hole. Part of this mystique was his charisma and his connection with the everyman, the blue-collar golfer. Palmer wore his emotions on his sleeve, and in stark contrast to today's PGA Tour golfing robots, you could tell how his round was going just by looking at him.

In the timeless classic *Golf in the Kingdom*, Michael Murphy, alluding to the power of intention, writes of "streamers of heart power for the ball to fly on. " That may be a bit of fanciful writing, but there is no question that intention and visualization play a big part in the success of many of the game's top performers. I witnessed, up close, a fascinating conversation late one evening on the practice tee at Lakewood during the New Orleans Open. I was watching Arnold Palmer and Doug Sanders winding up their practice session and there wasn't a lot of daylight left. They started fooling around hitting trick shots, making the ball curve in various ways, and hitting fades and draws simultaneously trying to get the balls to collide in midair (they actually did it twice!).

As they were finishing up and calling the caddies in (in those days the caddies would shag balls on the range), Palmer said to Sanders, "Doug, you know those vapor trails that the planes leave when the skies are clear? Well, I swear to you, sometimes as I'm setting up to a tee shot I look down the fairway and up in the air I can see the same sort of thing—like vapor trails—that recent drives have left in the air. So I just choose one that goes straight down the fairway and follow it with my drive. It's sort of like seeing the line of a putt."

He was serious, though I think Sanders was more than a little skeptical. But taking into consideration some of the amazing things that Arnold Palmer did on a golf course, there's no doubt that at least to him those lines were there!

Streamers of heart power? Maybe. Then again, maybe just pure, intense, focused powers of intention. Palmer sure seemed to have that.

Jack Nicklaus, on the other hand, had the same ability to focus at just the right time, but he went about his business in a more unemotional manner. Jack was Hoganlike in that regard and also, like Hogan, relied on supreme course management skills. Palmer was always aggressive, with a go-for-broke style that endeared him to his massive galleries, dubbed "Arnie's Army" by the media.

Hogan and Nicklaus won lots of tournaments with their minds, while Palmer won with his will and determination.

I saw many amazing things during my time at Lakewood observing the top players in action. I saw Gary Player and Nicklaus cold-top fairway woods, I saw Palmer throw a club à la Tommy Bolt, and I saw Lee Trevino win the New Orleans Open without making a bogey in the 72 holes of the tournament.

One year, in the heart of Palmer's prime, I saw a clear picture of the power of adrenaline. It was the first time I'd seen Palmer in person. It was my first year at Lakewood.

When he arrived on Tuesday afternoon (in his helicopter on the driving range), he got out carrying a briefcase, wearing grey slacks and a sportcoat and looking every bit like some James Bond type.

The first thing he did was to come into the golf shop and my first impression was that he didn't look nearly as big as I had envisioned my hero to be.

He greeted Jim and me, shaking our hands (as my hands were shaking), and after a little small talk headed over to the clubhouse for a quick lunch and then to the locker room to change clothes for a practice round. Palmer was so popular then that even his practice rounds drew enormous crowds.

Lakewood's pro shop had this huge picture window facing the first tee so I had a great view of Palmer arriving to tee off on the first hole. There must have been 5,000 members of Arnie's Army waiting.

All of a sudden, the crowd parted and here came Palmer, purposefully striding toward the tee, looking into the crowd and smiling.

As he walked out of the crowd and onto the first tee, I had to do a double take to make sure it was the same person that had been in the pro shop an hour earlier.

This guy was 2 inches taller and 20 pounds heavier, and his arms looked like a weightlifter's. He was literally pumped up!

It's adrenaline. It's having thousands of people cheering your every move and adoring you. Arnold Palmer literally fed off of the crowd's energy (love) and the crowd, in turn, fed off of his tremendous charisma.

There's never been another player so revered by the people, and there might never be another one loved so much.

Connie and I were at one of his last Masters appearances, and he could only take about a half swing and couldn't hit his drives 200 yards, but the thousands were still there. They didn't care. They just wanted to be there, in his presence.

At that same Masters, we were watching the par-3 tournament on Wednesday. We were behind the 8th tee, watching group after group come by. The hole was about 115 yards. In one group, Blaine McCallister hit his tee shot about 12 to 15 feet to the right of the hole, a pretty good shot.

There was a mild smattering of applause from the huge crowd. Blaine turned around, faced the crowd, and said, "If that had been Arnie, y'all would have gone wild!"

And with that, some guy stands up and yelled, "Yeah, Blaine, but *you* ain't Arnie!"

When it comes to golf, Arnie will *always* be the King.

I had one unexpected personal encounter with Arnie in 1975. I had made the cut in the New Orleans Open, and in those days if you made the cut in a tournament you were exempt from Monday qualifying for the next event. So I was exempt into the field at the Byron Nelson Classic at Preston Trails Country Club in Dallas.

After my practice round on Tuesday, late in the day, I was in the locker room washing my hands. As I turned to leave I saw Arnold Palmer sitting on the bench changing into his street shoes. There was no one else in the locker room. He looked up and said, "You must be a new player out here." I said, "Yes sir," and he extended his hand and said, "Arnold Palmer, good to meet you." (As if I didn't know who *he* was!)

So I told him my name and when he asked where I was from I said New Orleans. He said, "I really enjoy your town. I try not to ever miss playing there. Great hospitality, great food."

We made small talk for maybe 30 seconds and as he started to leave he said, "Son, if I can ever help you with anything let me know." I thanked him and told him that it was really great to meet him.

He walked away, but then turned and looked right into my eyes and said, "And I *really* mean that."

How classy is that? Arnold Palmer taking a few minutes to sincerely engage a star-struck rookie. The thing is, Palmer treats everybody like that.

If only the world was full of Arnold Palmers.

I got to play the first two rounds of the Magnolia Classic with Tom Watson in the early '70s. Hattiesburg Country Club is a pine tree forest and the fairways look like bowling lanes. When you play golf there it sounds like baseball spring training, with golf balls rattling off of the pines every few seconds. In the second round Watson hit six greens in regulation and shot 67. I hit 14 greens and shot 71. Maybe that's why he won nine Majors and I didn't.

Hattiesburg had a great barbecue place called the Wagon Wheel back then, and all of the players would flock there every night.

Fast forward to 2009 at Crooked Stick for the U.S. Senior Open. After a practice round I was coming out of the Taylor Made Tour Van and I encountered Watson. We chatted for a minute and I told him about playing with him at Hattiesburg almost 40 years earlier.

He said, "I wonder if the Wagon Wheel is still there?"

What a memory! That barbecue must have been pretty darn special—and I thought that Kansas City, where Watson is from, was famous for theirs!

Lee Trevino spotted me and a fellow rookie one day on the practice range at Preston Trail in Dallas. It was late afternoon and no one else was there. Trevino stopped hitting shots and came over and introduced himself, asking where we're from and so on.

He ended up spending more than an hour giving us tips about life on the tour, and even gave us some green-reading tips. No one ever knew it but us. He said to come to him if we needed any help with anything. He sure didn't have to do what he did.

Most of the guys on tour were very nice, and very willing to help young players. That's just the way it was. Sure, there were a few prima donnas who had overinflated egos and detested playing in pro-ams, but thankfully their numbers were few.

Those guys seemed oblivious to the fact that the pro-am amateurs and tournament volunteers were responsible for the prize money that was lining their pockets.

One year I was invited by Freddie Haas to play as his partner in a practice round for the New Orleans Open at Lakewood against Tom Weiskopf and Ed Sneed.

We were only playing a $10 Nassau, but you have to understand that Freddie was famous for being rather tight with the cash.

Weiskopf had a reputation for holing out more long shots from the fairway than perhaps any other player in history. It was just one of those strange, unexplainable things.

Anyway, we lost the front nine one down, but we were one up on the back nine coming to the 18th hole, which meant we were even for the whole match and if we tied the last hole, no money would change hands. Eighteen at Lakewood was a really good par-4 in those days, playing about 440 yards. Today's bombers would consider it fairly short.

We all hit the fairway but it was playing into the wind, probably playing more like 470. Ed and Freddie both bunkered their approach shots, and of course I was next as Weiskopf was a very long hitter.

I remember hitting a 4 wood and hit a really good, solid shot that ended up 20 to 25 feet pin high. Freddie came over, elated because his money seemed safe, and put his arm on my shoulder. He said, "Atta boy, pards, good shot!"

What happened next is burned in my memory. Weiskopf hit a 4 iron that never left the flag. It landed 15 feet or so short of the hole and ran straight into it as if it had eyes.

I look over at Freddie and he looked like he'd been punched in the stomach. I had to try hard to keep from laughing. You'd have thought that the $20 we'd lost had left him penniless.

Anyway, Weiskopf lived up to his reputation as a "hole-out" artist!

Incidentally, he had also chipped in once earlier in the round.

One year at Lakewood I'd made the cut with one under 143, but had a bad third round, shooting 75. I was tied for dead last with Hall of Famer Player and two-time major winner Tony Jacklin, who was having a bad week.

For the final round, because of an odd number of players, Jacklin and I were paired in just a twosome in the first tee time for Sunday's final round.

He was not happy, having to play with an unknown at the break of dawn. I, on the other hand, was excited to get to play with a player of his stature, figuring I would get to learn a lot by observing one of the game's top players close up.

Tony was not rude or anything, but he said virtually nothing, playing fast and obviously thinking about the airport.

Tony Jacklin and I played that final round in a couple of minutes short of two hours, walking.

Bob Roesler, the longtime sports editor of the *Times-Picayune*, the major New Orleans newspaper, wrote an article the next day titled "By Dawn's Early Light."

Roesler wrote about the round, and how it was the fastest round ever played on the PGA Tour. That record, as far as I know, still stands.

For the record, Jacklin shot 73 and I shot 74—not bad considering we virtually ran around the course.

I could go on with dozens of stories from my time on the tour, but that's not the purpose of this book.

I'd like to add one phrase to the ex-tour players' lament: "I left the tour with an empty money clip and a pocketful of memories—*and a thousand stories!*"

Someday I may write a book about all of the stories and experiences from a lifetime in golf, and include lots of unpublished Hogan stories, but that's not what this one's about.

This book is about the greatest ball striker in the history of golf, and how what he discovered about the golf swing can improve your swing and enhance your enjoyment of this incredible human activity.

Like Arnie says, "it's *the Greatest Game!*"

Gary Player

Gary Player from South Africa just might be the most underrated, or more appropriately the most underappreciated golfer in the history of golf.

A few years after I started playing golf and started following the pros on television every week, I adopted Gary Player as my golfing idol. It was because he was my size, and because he hit the ball the way that I wanted to hit it, with a right-to-left draw that would get extra roll. Like Player, I had to make up the distance deficit somehow. I even took to wearing all black, just like him. I didn't know it at the time, but I couldn't have chosen a better role model. My adulation back then was all golf related, but many years later that adulation turned to his many other positive attributes.

If it weren't for Arnold Palmer and Jack Nicklaus, whose combined long shadows shaded Player's presence on the game's biggest stages, Gary just might be at the top end of conversations about the greatest golfer ever.

Just look at his record:

PGA Tour—24 wins
Champions Tour—19 wins
Sunshine Tour—73 wins
Other tours—134 wins

Majors:
Masters—3 wins
U.S. Open—1 win
British Open—3 wins
PGA—2 wins
*World Golf Hall Of Fame Member

This amazing record was compiled by a man standing 5'7" and weighing 150 pounds.

His playing career has spanned 63 years and counting, and he has recorded victories in too many countries to list here.

In addition, he has been an outstanding ambassador for the game of golf globally, and single-handedly made physical fitness an integral part of every aspiring young golfer's regimen.

I had my first encounter with Player in 1974 at what was then the Danny Thomas Memphis Open. It was after the first round and I had just come out of the locker room. My four-year-old stepdaughter Kristen was there with her mother, and as I was picking her up Player came out of the locker room door. He said hi and started talking to her, asking her name and making small talk with us, asking where we're from and asking me how long I've been out on tour and such.

Then he picked Kristen up, sat on a bench just outside of the locker room, and spent at least 15 minutes talking to us.

At that time, much was made in the media about Player and his physical fitness routines and his emphasis on eating healthy foods. That kind of lifestyle was new to the Tour, which had always been famous for the "19th hole"—drinking and partying.

So I seized the opportunity to ask him this question: "What's the best exercise for golf?"

Here's what he said, and it's a tip for you as it was for me way back then. He said, "When you make a golf swing you use a very specific set of muscles. The only time that you use those particular muscles *all at the same time* is when you swing a golf club. If you swing a *weighted* club you are using those specific muscles but with added weight. In effect, you're performing *weightlifting for golf*, specifically."

I believe that swinging a weighted club was one of Gary Player's secrets for generating the power he did, which was considerable for a man his size. It probably also contributed to his golfing longevity by keeping his golf muscles toned and stretched.

It's a practice tool that I highly recommend.

A couple of times years later I encountered Player again at the PGA Merchandise Show in Orlando. I was signing my books for Booklegger, who was at the time the main distributor of golf books in the industry.

Connie was with me both times and when we spotted Player she wanted to meet him. Gary is a real charmer and the ladies love him. For that matter, so do men!

Anyway, the first year that I ran into him at the show I introduced Connie to him and recounted the story from Memphis years ago. Of course he couldn't have remembered that but you'd never know it. We talked like old friends and lamented getting older and losing distance off the tee.

Along those lines, Gary is famous for saying that he knew that it was time to retire when he could *hear* his drives land!

He is so gracious and treats everyone with the utmost respect.

In my book Gary Player is right up there with Palmer when it comes to charisma, and certainly right up there with Palmer and Nicklaus when it comes to legendary status as a player.

NOTES ON PUTTING

PUTTING JUST MIGHT be the most mystifying part of golf. Any serious golfer has experienced it: some days everything goes in, but most of the time the hole seems to be covered in cellophane. Some days you can clearly see the line, and yet most of the time you struggle to read putts.

Why is this? It's a question that has gone unanswered, at least to the extent of offering a permanent solution.

Throughout the long history of golf there have been many great putters, players whose expertise on the greens has stood the test of time. But even they have experienced those days when the hole seems smaller and elusive.

Many experts have said that great putters are born, that you can't turn a bad putter into a great one. I believe that. Putting requires great feel and touch.

And yet I also believe that a bad putter can become a fairly decent one with practice and proper tutelage.

If I ask you to toss a rubber ball to me from 20 feet away and you consistently toss it over my head or at my feet, you're not going to be a good putter. But with lots of long-term practice you can get somewhat better.

But let's say you have good natural feel and touch, but you still struggle. What can you do to make more putts?

The best putters throughout history have all had different styles. They grip the putter in different ways, they stand in various postures, their putting strokes are different.

So what are the things that they have in common, besides making tons of putts?

1. **They *reach* the hole consistently.** Their distance control, because they have good natural feel and touch, is consistent. They have also developed a consistent stroke with regard to contacting the ball on the sweet spot most of the time. This helps immensely with distance control. (To determine your putter's sweet spot, just bounce a golf ball against the face until you feel the most "solid" spot.)

2. **They seem to always have the ball approaching the hole from the high side.** They play more break, generally, than a poor putter. Poor putters tend to severely underread the break.

3. **They *roll* the ball, they don't "hit" it.**

4. **They like their putters.** Their putters look good to them, and they feel good in their hands.

5. **Good putters remain confident at all times, on every putt.** Like an NFL cornerback, they have short memories when it comes to failures.

All that being said, how can a poor putter improve?

By following the above principles, a poor putter can get better. If distance control is an issue, drills can improve touch. One drill is to find a 20- to 25-foot putt on the practice green between two holes that is fairly straight and somewhat downhill. Take a couple of balls and practice going back and forth between the holes, rolling downhill to one hole and then turning around and putting back up the hill. By going back and forth, alternating downhill and uphill putts, you will eventually improve your feel for distance control.

Another drill is to lay the flagstick or an alignment rod two feet behind the hole and go back to about 25 feet and start rolling putts, trying to reach the hole but not going as far past as the flagstick or alignment rod.

You can always get better, but consistently great putters are a rare breed. No matter how good your mechanics and natural feel are, putting is still an inexact science. It's part art and part science, just like ball striking, and a ball rolling on a grass surface is always going to be at the mercy of the terrain. Small imperfections, insects, tiny pieces of debris from trees—all of these things can deflect a perfectly struck putt.

But by practicing and following the above principles, you can maximize your chances for making putts.

Hogan and Putting

Hogan did not love putting like he loved controlling golf shots. I believe that the reason was that he *could* control his shots, but the *result* of his putts was something that was out of his control.

More than once he publicly said that putting should be abolished, that there should be no hole, just a flagstick, and that points should be awarded for both hitting the green in regulation and proximity to the flagstick.

Confirming my belief is what he told one of my early mentors, Freddie Haas, when Freddie offered some putting advice to Hogan at a time when Ben was struggling on the greens. I alluded to this comment earlier, which also was recorded in Mike Towle's book *I Remember Ben Hogan*, a book of short stories by people who knew or competed against Hogan. Hogan told Freddie, "I don't want to be remembered as a great putter, only as a great ball striker."

Nonetheless, in his prime Ben Hogan was a very good putter. Because he hit so many greens in regulation and had so many birdie opportunities from six to 30 feet, it seemed like he missed a lot of putts, which of course he did. But you don't shoot thousands of rounds in the mid to high 60s, as Hogan did in his career, without making a lot of birdie putts.

As he got older his putting skills diminished, as happens to most players, and people tend to overdo describing his late-career struggles.

In the end, though, it remains a mystery why putting success seems to come and go randomly. Is it a matter of optics, or the effects of the way light plays on different surfaces at various times of the day?

Or is it the fact that we're human, and our feel and touch change day to day?

Who knows, but I don't think that Hogan's wish will ever be granted. Putting is here to stay.

Arnold Palmer had a humorous and interesting observation once when someone was lamenting birdie putts lipping out. The person said, "If only the hole were 6 inches wider!" Palmer said, "If it were, you'd still be complaining about 30-footers lipping out instead of 10-footers"!

One great putting tip: in a poor putting stroke, the player's left wrist breaks down on the through stroke. This happens because the shoulders stop and the putter decelerates and the left wrist breaks down. To cure this, keep the right shoulder moving on the through stroke. If you do, the left wrist will not break down.

/

CLOSING NOTES

Hogan Fans

Around the world, Ben Hogan fans number in the tens of thousands. They are as interested in him as much as ever, and maybe even more as his legend grows.

What exactly is it that spurs such widespread, longtime interest?

It can't be just his ball-striking mastery, as others have reached high levels of such efficiency, though perhaps not quite on the same high level that Hogan achieved.

Perhaps it's his killer competitive drive, or his solitary, secret persona. Or to some his passion and devotion to plain old hard work that was validated and rewarded with great success.

And maybe it's the story of how he overcame catastrophic adversity in his life, after witnessing, as a young boy, his father's suicide, and how he survived a near-fatal car crash and defied all logic and professional medical opinion by not only recovering but elevating his performance.

Fueling this phenomenon of widespread, longtime interest is definitely the mystery of his secret, and the six-decades-long search for answers.

I hope that this book has put an end to that search, but there will probably still be those who want to continue the search just because they enjoy that process, just like some people want to figure out their golf swings on their own, ignoring the advice of even top-notch teaching professionals.

Hogan fans are worldwide, and span age groups from teenagers to octogenarians.

Close to home, I relate this story of one longtime fan whose illustrious career as a teacher and clubfitting expert has been deeply affected by the Hogan mystique.

The PGA director of golf at my home club, James Leitz, is a *Golf Digest* top 50 teacher, a *Golf Magazine* top 100 teacher, and a *Golf Digest* top 100 clubfitter.

James told me this story about his early exposure to Hogan and his fascination with the Hogan mystique.

He said it was early in his career, 1982, and he had acquired a 16 mm copy of the famous episode of *Shell's Wonderful World of Golf* featuring Ben Hogan versus Sam Snead. The match was held in May of 1964 at Houston Country Club in Houston, Texas.

In that match Ben Hogan hit every fairway and all 18 greens in regulation. He had makeable birdie putts on nearly every hole. It was a stunning display of laserlike accuracy and textbook shotmaking.

James had to rent a projector in order to view the tape, and he remembers setting the projector up on his bed (his space was limited) and showing the tape on the white wall of the bedroom of his trailer.

Seeing Hogan's ability to completely control the golf ball hooked him to an admiration for Hogan that has lasted throughout his career. Indeed, his office at the club and his office at his teaching center are both adorned with all sorts of Hogan memorabilia and photographs. Such is the puzzling nature of the way that golfers get caught up in admiration for Ben Hogan.

The global appeal for the man's near mastery of perhaps the most difficult game stretches across oceans and continents, and even crosses the bridge between fact and fiction.

Hogan's secret, enduring six decades of wild speculation, also appears in works of fiction, as pointed out to me by my longtime friend Tony Schueler.

Witness what was written in the *The Greatest Course That Never Was* (J. Michael Veron, 2001) on page 172:

"I don't suppose Hogan let you in on the 'secret' that he supposedly had about the golf swing."

"He didn't tell me anythin' except 'bout rakin' a bunker, but I heard him say somethin' to Mr. Jones that was interestin'."

"What's that?"

"He said that the one thing he worked on the most was keepin' his right knee from movin' durin' the swing."

I wonder where Veron got that from, yet another feature of Hogan's technique that even in fiction purports to reveal the secret!

To the Reader/Golfer:

Work with Hogan's geometry through drills and repetitions, and get your swing on track. Eliminate your compensations and in-swing adjustments and you'll realize a new consistency and effortless power. Your enjoyment of this amazing game will be enhanced and your scores will dramatically improve.

Best of luck on and off the course! And don't forget to smile.

Author's Note:

As I put the finishing touches on this book, the golfing world has suffered an immeasurable loss. Arnold Palmer, the King, has passed away at age 87. The world of golf will never be the same, and I feel as if a part of my youth went with him. Arnie—RIP and thank you!

ABOUT THE AUTHOR

LARRY MILLER IS a life member of the PGA of America and a former PGA Tour player. He is the author of three other books on golf and performance and has taught golf and given talks and clinics all over the United States and abroad. He lives in Mandeville, Louisiana, a suburb of New Orleans.